T0383193

BRINGING JOBS BACK TO THE USA

TO THE USA

Rebuilding America's Manufacturing
through Reshoring

Bringing Jobs Back to the USA

Rebuilding America's Manufacturing through Reshoring

Tim Hutzel • Dave Lippert

CRC Press
Taylor & Francis Group
Boca Raton London New York

CRC Press is an imprint of the
Taylor & Francis Group, an **informa** business

A PRODUCTIVITY PRESS BOOK

CRC Press
Taylor & Francis Group
6000 Broken Sound Parkway NW, Suite 300
Boca Raton, FL 33487-2742

© 2014 by Tim Hutzel and Dave Lippert
CRC Press is an imprint of Taylor & Francis Group, an Informa business

No claim to original U.S. Government works

Printed on acid-free paper
Version Date: 20140514

International Standard Book Number-13: 978-1-4665-5756-7 (Hardback)

Visit the Taylor & Francis Web site at
http://www.taylorandfrancis.com

and the CRC Press Web site at
http://www.crcpress.com

Contents

SECTION IV   The Reshoring Trend

SECTION V   A Decision-Making
Model to Reshore...or Not

SECTION VI   Making the Decision
to Reshore Is Just the Beginning

SECTION VII Looking into the Future

Foreword

Growing up in the 1970s, I was a fan of the *Little House on the Prairie* TV series, which was very popular in those days. I remember an episode vividly, in which Charles Ingalls builds a rocking chair with all the craftsmanship he can bring to the project. At the end of the episode, the setting moves forward a century in time to show the chair—now a prized antique—in the hands of contemporary collectors. As the camera pans closer to the chair, a signature becomes visible: "Charles Ingalls." Even as a little boy, watching what I knew was a fictional scene, I was moved by the idea that someone could build something that would stand the test of time, a statement of excellence for generations to come.

The author of the "Little House" series of books, Laura Ingalls Wilder, lived long enough to see the end of World War II and the emergence of the United States as a global leader in manufacturing. Throughout much of the twentieth century, our country simply assumed that we would always be a leading global manufacturer, and that this would be a heritage we would pass on from generation to generation. How dangerous can our assumptions be? How quickly can pride become our downfall?

In the early decades of the twenty-first century, the United States finds itself in a quandary. We have offshored manufacturing for short-term financial efficiencies, while jeopardizing part of our long-term strategic standing in the world. Where the United States loses domestic manufacturing capability, we risk vulnerability should world conditions ever disrupt the offshored manufacturing on which a significant portion of our economy depends. Ultimately, the competitiveness of our manufacturing sector is only as strong as its weakest link.

I also believe there is an even deeper, more profound issue with the trend toward offshoring. I believe that God created every one of us for a purpose in life and that, for some of our citizens, purposeful work is in the manufacturing sector. When our society loses manufacturing opportunities, we lose vocational variety. We lose part of our quality of work life as a nation. My heart is for a nation where our citizens have ready access to any vocation—any call of God for our work—whether that field of work is manufacturing or any other vocation.

In this timely and thoughtful book, Tim Hutzel and Dave Lippert bring reshoring to life in purposeful and practical terms. Unlike many authors who introduce a concept and inspire a readership, but ignore the details, Hutzel and Lippert bring a precision of presentation that one would expect of master practitioners in manufacturing.

What strikes me the most is that reshoring has the potential to become a movement of its own. If we so choose, it has the potential to become a "priority in practice" for our country. Imagine if our government leaders made reshoring more than a talking point. Imagine if our business leaders made reshored products a preference in their purchasing. Imagine if our educational leaders made reshoring a cause for college and graduate students.

A movement needs a cause, and domestic manufacturing certainly meets that requirement. A movement needs leadership, and Tim Hutzel, Dave Lippert, and others are boldly stepping forward to seize this moment. A movement needs followers and that depends upon the focus and commitment of our citizens. It won't happen by accident. It will happen by design and by diligence. Reshoring needs to be embraced as a concept across broad sectors of our society.

I encourage you to read this book not only as a primer on reshoring, but also as a point of inception for your engagement in the movement. How can you share the message of reshoring in your sphere of influence? How can you encourage decision makers and influencers to rally for reshoring? In essence, how can you make a difference?

We are beginning to see a small shift toward reshoring, and this is encouraging. Just as the first revolution of a flywheel is the most difficult, we have some of the "start-up" momentum we need to bring reshoring up to full speed. The challenge before us is daunting, so we need to keep the vision behind this reshoring movement on our minds and in our hearts.

I believe that as our country begins to reshore, we will begin to restore… to restore strategic strength as a manufacturing force, to restore economic resilience as better paying jobs are brought back home, to restore competitive positioning for future marketplace opportunities, to restore vocational fulfillment for citizens gifted in manufacturing, and much more. As the famous sociologist Margaret Mead once commented, "Never doubt that a small group of thoughtful, committed citizens can change the world. Indeed, it is the only thing that ever has."

Chuck Proudfit

President, At Work on Purpose (http://atworkonpurpose.org/)
"Mobilizing the Work World for Christ"
Cincinnati, Ohio

President, SkillSource Consulting (http://skillsource.com/)
Cultivating Purpose Powered™ Performance by "Unleashing the
Organization" to Fully Realize Inherent Potential
Cincinnati, Ohio

Preface

WHY WE WROTE THIS BOOK

We wrote this book because we believe the trend in American jobs being exported (offshored) to China, Mexico, Vietnam, Bangladesh, India, and many other countries is making America weaker. Here are some examples of what America is experiencing in 2014, the year this book was published:

High unemployment
Low economic growth
Lost tax revenue
Low national income
High national debt, especially to China
Risks to defense if our country faces another global war
High welfare
Low world prestige
Scarcity of apprentice programs
Lost job skills
Trend toward becoming a service-focused country
Lack of part-time and summer jobs
Lost opportunities for young people to learn basic job practices
High personal student loan debt
Hard work frowned upon by too many Americans
"Made in America" products harder to find
Lower national pride
Trend toward higher social welfare
Judeo–Christian work ethic floundering

American manufacturers have also been affected by offshoring:
Weakened supply chains
New employees with poor basic job skills
Difficult to find employees with manufacturing skills

Loss of business-to-business customers

Products copied by offshored suppliers

Forced to compete with similar products with artificially low prices made offshore

Loss of control of production processes

Loss of control of materials' supply chain

Loss of controlling quality at offshored supplier

Customer complaints of poor quality

Returned goods by unhappy customers

High warranty claims

Offhour conference calls with offshored suppliers in different time zones

Differences in languages

Differences in cultures

Inadvertently supporting the use of child labor

Inadvertently supporting poor environmental practices

High-cost and time-consuming transcontinental flights and visits to offshored suppliers

Large order quantities

Long lead times

Unfavorable purchasing terms

High shipping costs

High trucking costs

Transportation damage costs and issues

Storage costs and issues of high-volume order quantities

Capital tied up in offshored materials and orders

Less flexibility responding to market changes

Longer time to get product changes to market

Long cash-conversion cycles

Customers wanting more "made in America" products

Economic changes such as higher wages in China and higher transportation costs have begun a shift in offshoring to bring back (reshore) American manufacturing. Some companies have already begun to reshore some or all of their products:

General Electric—water heaters

Master Lock—locks

Wham-O®—Frisbee™

Suarez—space heaters

Michigan Ladders—fiberglass ladders

Chesapeake Bay Candle—candles
Neutex—television assembly
Seesmart—LED lights
Coleman—coolers
Horton Archery—bows
Tacony—vacuum cleaners
Outdoor Great Room—furniture
All Clad—kitchenware

The trend is in the right direction, but it is not moving fast enough! We want to change that. We are committed to our vision and mission.

Our vision: "America will regain its prominence in the world as the premier manufacturing and service provider with all American citizens' engagement and support."

Our mission: "We will provide education, training, and involvement to American manufacturers to help them make the best decisions regarding reshoring their products back to America."

We hope you enjoy our book and decide to take at least the initial steps toward reshoring that we have put forward.

Tim Hutzel
Oxford, Ohio

Dave Lippert
Hamilton, Ohio

Acknowledgments

This book has been a 2-year work in process, but actually it began a year earlier when Tim Hutzel said to his friend, Dave Lippert, "Hey! I've got an idea." Those were words of caution for Dave. He knew that when Tim had an idea, work and, sometimes, controversy were certain to follow. Tim had been consulting to Dave's company, Hamilton Caster, since 1996 and was always coming up with ideas, most of them good.

Tim had recently finished his book, *Keeping Your Business in the U.S.A.: Profit Globally While Operating Locally*. The book is a history of several American manufacturers, including Hamilton Caster, telling how they managed to stay in business by implementing simple manufacturing and business techniques to keep their manufacturing in America. Tim's research while writing the book exposed him and Dave to many companies that kept their work here and many that sent their manufacturing overseas. Tim and Dave were alarmed by the trend in exporting jobs because of the negative fallout to America. They wanted to do something to stop the off-shoring and they began a campaign to turn the tide. Tim and Dave made reshoring presentations to leaders in business, manufacturing, communities, professional societies, education, and anyone they thought could help. They were running out of steam, funds, and time to make the presentations and for a while everything came to a halt. Then, Tim had an idea.

His idea was to reach more people by writing a book that not only told the story of offshoring and what it was doing to America, but also instructed readers how to bring their manufacturing back home. Dave agreed, and that started the ball of researching for 1 year and then the writing began. With the writing came advising, reviewing, critiquing, recommending, and sometimes arguing by a team of people chosen by Tim and Dave for their expertise and interest in reshoring and America's future. Dave and Tim want to acknowledge their team for their assistance in producing this book.

In alphabetical order, a grateful "thank-you" is given to the following:

> Ken Campbell has over 45 years of business and manufacturing experience. His last engagement was as a product quality engineer at GE Aviation. Ken reviewed every word that was written by Tim and Dave and provided valuable input to the models.

Rachel Campbell provided a keen eye to catch all the errors in writing and grammar and ensured the *P*s and *Q*s were in proper order. Many thanks to Rachel.

Jim Cashell is a retired business professor from Miami University who listened many evenings to Tim Hutzel's progress on the book and gave encouragement and advice that Tim most often took.

Kenny Craig is the CEO of the Hamilton Ohio Chamber of Commerce. Kenny's role as a general community business leader helped form the viewpoint needed to speak to Chamber of Commerce leaders.

Anne Eiting-Klamar is president and CEO of Midmark, the company that manufactures and sells exceptional equipment for doctors, dentists, and veterinarians. Anne is constantly on the road, as are many CEOs, and has very little time to give, except for company and family. Yet, Anne gave her time, graciously reading whatever documents were sent for her review. Her business viewpoint as a CEO has been very helpful.

Ray Gorman, the interim dean of Miami University's Farmer School of Business, sat with Tim on many occasions helping refine some of the business models used in the book.

Bruce Gray has 45 years of manufacturing experience in many different industries. His reviews helped shape the general form of the book and especially how it relates to the general manufacturing person.

Janet Haisley was a supervisor at Huffy Bicycles in Celina, Ohio, when the Chinese flooded the market with underpriced and undercosted bicycles. Her stories and insight into what happened before and after the Chinese invasion were extremely valuable.

Denny Knigga is a veteran manufacturer and has worked in supervision, engineering, and management for many companies. Denny's input came from his practical viewpoint.

Tom Lippert is the past vice president of Hamilton Caster and has many decades of experience that were shared to assist with the book. Tom's experience in marketing was especially helpful.

Mark Lohmann, the controller at Hamilton Caster, provided his time and financial expertise to improve the calculations in the reshoring decision-making model, which was extremely helpful.

Rocky Newman is a supply chain professor at Miami University's Farmer School of Business in Oxford, Ohio. Rocky conducted many mentoring sessions, which resulted in refining the decision-making models. He also gave freely of his time to observe the authors testing aspects of the model at on-site companies.

Joe Patten is the chairman of MainStream GS, a global service company providing solutions and action. Joe has been deeply involved with "you must make your products in China if we are going to sell them" situations. He understands what "made in China" can do to the company, the environment, and our country. Joe was continually supportive and served as a valuable sounding board.

Bob Wheeler is the president of Airstream, the premier RV manufacturer. Bob has lived the experience of transforming Airstream to a complete Lean system. He knows the effort and commitment it takes. He also knows the rewards that it brings. Bob's comments and critiques were useful in refining the Lean conversions sections.

Craig Vander Leest is a financial management professional who understands that the total financial picture is what really counts. Craig was helpful in refining our thought process and validating our methodologies.

Marc Wolfrum, vice president of Cincinnati Sub-Zero Medical, has been fortunate to lead many different operations for over 30 years. Marc also has experience leading companies in Lean transformations. His input shaped the presentation of many of the transformation topics.

The authors also want to thank their wives for their patience and understanding during the 3 years it took to write this book, so a special "thank you" to Cheryle Hutzel and Teresa Lippert!

Section I

The Story of Reshoring

1

Why Companies Offshore

Ever since the Great Recession, business sections of newspapers and numerous other media outlets have focused on the nagging unemployment problem in the United States. Though the economy has improved considerably, the unemployment rate has been frustratingly slow to drop. Some observers are saying it will take years, and others suggest it is systemic and may never return to prerecession "acceptable" levels. Most of these discussions eventually reach the manufacturing employment piece that has resulted from decades of moving work offshore, including entire factories and millions of jobs.

International trade has flourished for thousands of years, normally to the mutual benefit of all trading partners. Countries have natural and cultural advantages to make or produce certain goods, and can gain by trading these with countries that have advantages in other areas. Examples include those with climates favoring certain crop production or natural resources (e.g., oil) that others simply do not have. A somewhat recent phenomenon has been the accessing of relatively inexpensive and abundant labor to manufacture products that most often are returned to the offshoring country for use/sale. In other words, it has become attractive to send raw materials or parts to a country with low labor costs, have them assembled into finished products, and then return them to the country of origin. Even with the shipping costs to move the material halfway around the world and back, many US companies have rationalized an economic justification for doing this.

Transportation and technology have teamed up to facilitate this movement. Transoceanic shipping has become faster and more dependable and intercontinental communications have become easier. Offshoring has flourished. The sailing ships and early steamers from history, many of which were lost in storms and now decorate ocean floors as destinations for treasure hunters and scuba divers, gave way to the modern megatransports that carry incredible loads over thousands of miles. The piracy that threatened oceanic transportation not too many years ago is virtually nonexistent. Cellular communication and conference calls have enabled real-time communications across the globe, albeit with significant time of day challenges.

While the genesis of this modern offshoring movement may have seemed somewhat innocent, the level playing field that many businesses seek vanished (if it ever existed) amid countries vying for trade advantages. Some countries went well beyond the tax differences and trade barriers that naturally vary from country to country. They embraced policies that tilted the landscape significantly in their favor. They could provide substantial governmental support to entire industries, offering financial advantages unavailable in the United States due to its laissez-faire policies. With many of the special insider advantages invisible to those outside their country's borders, government-favored industries suddenly looked incredibly appealing to the international business community. Offshoring looked pretty good to many US manufacturers. Additionally, currency-fixing practices dramatically altered the relative currency values between competing countries, providing another avalanche of financial advantages for some. Free market economies suffered when their governments refused to play this game (for many good reasons). In some cases, very disparate trade barriers to imports aided a country's home industry by raising massive bureaucratic and other hurdles to international competitors.

The initial results of offshoring—consumer products that showed up on store shelves with lower price tags—initially looked attractive to the US buying public. Items like radios, televisions, and bicycles were instant bargains. The standard of living seemed to escalate as every family could buy more and more "stuff" simply because prices were so low. The amount of clothing, shoes, electronic devices, and toys owned today by the average American family was not even imagined 50 years ago. Part of the reason this is true is because of the offshoring phenomenon.

An article detailing iconic American products no longer produced in America described the impact on the consumer as production of goods was shifted to lower cost countries. One example of these products is bicycles. A market formerly dominated by American manufacturer Huffy, the production shifted to China as lower prices to consumers completely changed the game. In fact, China exported bikes to other countries besides the United States, including Japan, South Korea, and Australia. One quote summed up the major reason for this shift: "Today, a standard fireball-red Huffy bike made in China sells for $40 at Wal-Mart—about 50% less than what it cost when Huffy was in Celina, Ohio."[1]

In 2004, when the report was made, this was possible in China because workers received free housing and earned only a pittance compared to their American counterparts. At that time, Chinese workers earned as little as $0.25 per hour!

Levi Strauss, the famed maker of blue jeans, started shifting its production from the United States to Third World countries in the 1990s to escape high wages in a very competitive market. By the middle of the first decade in the new millennium, every Levi sewing plant in the United States had been shuttered, costing thousands of sewing and other jobs. Yet, for the typical consumer of blue jeans, this was great news since it meant considerably lower prices. Lower prices meant either more jeans or more of something else with the money saved.

Sports helmets, worn by bicycle riders of all ages, as well as many players in other sports, were another product that saw production shift mostly to Asia. Except for a few sources in Italy and Germany, one is most likely to find a "made in China" or "made in Taiwan" label on helmets. Ironically, the considerably lower prices may account for the increased usage of this safety equipment.

Yet an ugly side effect from all the offshoring, initially unnoticed by most people, began to emerge. Factories full of good-paying jobs relocated to Third World countries to take advantage of the cheap labor and US families began to feel the pinch of the lost jobs and reduced incomes. Somewhat masked for a while by the trend of two-income families, this assault on family income has outgrown even the potential of two-income families to keep pace. For a number of reasons, but due in part to offshoring, the next generation of Americans is not expected to have a standard of living equal to or better than their parents'.

When an increasing number of people either do not have jobs or do not have better paying manufacturing jobs, the standard of living is bound to decrease. One measurement of the standard of living is personal disposable income. Due partly to the Great Recession and also to the dearth of good jobs in its wake, US disposable personal income dropped after 2008, and even 3 years later was still 4% below the 2008 peak. For the average household, this meant a loss of almost $1,600 spending dollars annually. A Michigan family serves as an example of this. Sadly, this type of story is repeated too often these days and in large measure is due to the shift of manufacturing to other countries[2]:

> In Royal Oak, Mich., Adam Kowal knows exactly how the squeeze feels. After losing a warehouse job in Lansing, he, his wife, and their two children have had little recourse but to move in with his mother. Now working at a school cafeteria, Mr. Kowal earns 28 percent less than at his last job.
>
> He and his wife now eat out once a month instead of once a week, do no socializing, and eat less expensive foods, such as ground chuck instead of ground sirloin. "My mom was hoping her kids would lead a better life than her, but so far that has not happened," says Kowal.

Economic collateral damage began to grow. Breadwinners lost jobs and either joined the unemployment ranks or were frequently forced to accept lower paying jobs. As a result, they paid less tax to all levels of government. In many cases, the unemployed placed increasing demands on existing programs designed to help those who struggle. Many of these government-sponsored programs depended on taxes, which were negatively impacted by the lost jobs! To some extent, everything supported by taxes suffered some loss. In fact, the negatives snowballed as more displaced workers created increasing demands on the system while the system received decreasing revenue needed to provide support. By one account, large US multinational companies have offshored as many as 2.9 million jobs during the past 10 years. The tax impact from that loss, felt at all levels from federal to local, is huge.

Playing with some real numbers exposes the magnitude of the impact on the US Treasury. During a 10-year period, approximately 2.9 million jobs were lost. Assuming the average annual pay from manufacturing jobs was $43,000 and the personal income tax on these incomes was 20%, the loss to tax collections was about $25 billion each year. Staggering—and yet this represents only the federal tax loss. State and local losses would be considerable as well.[3]

The auto industry all by itself created a major vacuum of tax revenue in some locations as plants closed due primarily to the influx of imports. The higher the concentration of manufacturing jobs was in one locale, the more devastating was the impact when the jobs were lost. It was something akin to the "all eggs in one basket" phenomenon. When times were good, they were very good. But when they turned bad, they went very badly. "One company" towns, where employment was dominated by one company, suffered the most. In some cases, even the local schools suffered significant loss of resources. The May 12, 2006, issue of *Executive Intelligence Review* explained it with several concrete examples[4]:

> The imminent closing of Saginaw, Michigan's remaining two parts plants, for example, lays off the equivalent of 10% of the city's shrinking population, and takes away even more of its tax base. The school system revenues of two Ohio cities, Batavia and Sharonville, are knocked down 30% by the closing of a Batavia plant.

The damage did not end with public support system revenue declines. The tsunami of cheap imported products impacted local business economies in at least two ways. First, those who lost their jobs had less family disposable income with which to support the local service industry. Everyone from hairdressers to haberdashers (well, maybe not so much the haberdashers!) saw impact on their business. Restaurants had less traffic. The same was true for movie theaters, roller skating rinks, and many others. Some of these businesses did not survive and closed as a result. Then there was even more demand on the support system! Maytag's plant closing in Galesburg, Illinois, in 2004 provides a vivid example of how this "trickle down" impact happens. In that case, one plant closing cost 1,600 jobs, or nearly 5% of the local workforce. When the dust had settled, two local jobs were eliminated for each manufacturing position lost.[5]

In 2012 Whirlpool Corporation closed its factory in Benton Harbor, Michigan, the home of its headquarters. Impact was felt at many levels, including a hair salon. Personal stories highlight the reality.

"Whirlpool just closed a factory, and that hurt my business, my little business. I lost a lot of clients," said Mary Alice Adams, who runs a hair salon in Benton Harbor.[6]

Second, the departed factories left a ripple effect on the local or regional commercial business economies. Every factory depended on a number of local resources for support. For example, factories with metalworking used tooling suppliers, and perhaps weld equipment suppliers. Then there were equipment repair services, parts providers, roof repair and replacement, landscapers, paved surface providers, and typically a long list of other local vendors that depended somewhat on the factory that was now relocated overseas. Perhaps to a greater degree than the impact on the displaced factory workers, these ripples hit hard. Now there were even more unemployed workers. The Galesburg, Illinois, saga of 1,600 job losses spread well beyond the direct impact of the unemployed Maytag workers. A local steel building plant employing 270 closed its doors shortly after the Maytag plant, and a number of other businesses reduced their workforces to adjust to decreased demand.[5]

Newton, Iowa, the home of Maytag's headquarters, saw devastation of its local economy when the giant company left town. This included a local advertising agency, which had held the Maytag account for many years. In fact, after 22 years of steady growth—while Maytag was in town— the firm took a major downward turn beginning when Maytag closed up shop in 2007. The advertising agency employee head count dropped from 22 employees to 10.[7] This serves as but one example of a local firm that extended the job losses well beyond the headline-grabbing Maytag Corporation. Others followed a similar pattern.

In some cases this led to a nationwide depletion of certain skills. One prominent example is tool and die work. Long a mainstay in the metal-working industry, tool and die workers spent a lifetime learning and then practicing their trade making the tooling used in the manufacturing process. The rush of factories to resettle overseas left many of these trades-people with no work; the younger apprentices saw a dead-end career and made appropriate life changes into other jobs. Many other manufacturing skills faded and are now lacking as some manufacturing begins to return to the United States. But the damage was done by the tidal wave of factory relocations overseas. This is yet another example of collateral damage created by excessive offshoring.

The auto industry has traditionally been a major employer of tool and die workers. By 2006, General Motors had reduced its workforce of 1,600 in the tool and die centers by over 300, and the company expected to further diminish the numbers to around 750. Key suppliers to General Motors were following that same pattern, dropping the skilled ranks by half or more.[4] Sadly, the same phenomenon has been occurring in the aerospace industry. The skill has been mostly relegated to small local machine shops and may be on its way out of the United States entirely. This is not because the skill is no longer necessary; rather, it is because jobs in our country are not supporting it.

Why did so many companies choose the pathway of moving production offshore? It is not surprising that there were many reasons, some of which developed over time. The most obvious answer is cost. Companies saw an opportunity to reduce the cost significantly (at least, so they thought) of products they sold in the United States In a move similar to buying material from a different vendor to achieve a cost reduction, these companies made a much bigger move to buy labor from a different vendor and achieve a sizable cost reduction. In some cases, where a favorable currency exchange rate and other government-controlled factors existed, the cost gap looked like a canyon. It seemed to make no sense NOT to offshore.

Levi Strauss is a household name around the planet. Many people wearing the famous apparel probably do not know where their clothing was made. More than a decade ago the company employed thousands in its US manufacturing, but almost all of that has shifted overseas. San Antonio was the site of some of the last remaining sewing plants in the United States, and two plants in that city along with three in Canada closed in 2003, adding almost 2,000 workers to unemployment lines.[8] Asia and Latin America benefited at North America's expense. This was a pattern that did not begin and end with Levi Strauss. Most of the apparel industry moved offshore before Levi did.

There were other incentives to move besides lower labor costs. In most overseas situations, particularly Third World countries, the environmental and safety laws are considerably looser than in the United States. A manufacturing process that is inherently dangerous either to workers or to the environment can have considerably less "legal oversight" overseas. In their exuberance to provide jobs for their citizens, many countries ignore their own environments. Moving a plant for this reason may boost earnings and shareholder value, but should disturb personal conscience.

Whirlpool, for example, cited the excessive costs of environmental compliance as a significant factor in the decision to relocate manufacturing overseas. At one point in the late 1990s, Whirlpool had spent about $30 million on pollution control equipment and anticipated spending another $9 million over the next 6 years. When the compliance costs are that significant, companies make decisions to relocate where they will not have those costs. This is not necessarily an indicator that the relocating company does not care about the environment. It might mean that it simply cannot compete with competitors who do not share the same cost structure. Compliance costs can make it an easier decision to move. In 1979 Whirlpool spent more than $20 million on governmental compliance, of which $3 million was for EPA matters and more than $1 million was Occupational Safety and Health Administration (OSHA)-related cost.[9]

Labor and safety issues may be either simpler or nonexistent overseas. In the United States employers must prepare for OSHA, EEOC (Equal Employment Opportunity Commission), NLRB (National Labor Relations

Board), and numerous state, regional, and local rules and regulations. This means many hours of management or consultant time and many dollars of added costs to comply. Moving a questionable manufacturing operation offshore to a country with few or no regulations can be very attractive. Whether or not the regulations in question are reasonable or necessary is not normally the issue. It can simply boil down to cost and reduced interference from the government. A 2004 report cited one of many examples of this:

> AXT Inc. is closing its gallium arsenide wafer facility in Fremont, Calif., and is shifting production to China. The plant was cited for dozens of violations for exposing employees to up to 31 times the amount of arsenic allowed. "Now AXT will be able to expose Chinese workers to the same toxic chemicals without fear of OSHA investigations or media exposures," says the report.[10]

Unintended consequences are those consequences that are unanticipated and, normally, very undesirable. For example, a local engineer in Hamilton, Ohio, suffered nagging dermatitis from handling parts sourced overseas. In a somewhat humorous but costly situation, a manufacturing plant found itself with a flea infestation inside the building! Apparently fleas entered via some overseas shipping containers made of wood. It required some special treatment to eliminate the pests and restore the workplace. Recently, a major auto manufacturer experienced so many quality defects in an expensive brand that it essentially quarantined the launch of a new model until final inspections could be made. Indeed, import news is not always good.

Besides these quirky consequences, it is perhaps most aggravating that many companies do not involve their own internal key functions to determine actual costs to import. Far too many importing manufacturers do not engage their sales, operations, production control, engineering, or purchasing departments prior to making offshoring decisions. When a company imports product, it impacts much more than the direct labor eliminated from the manufacturing process. Engineering struggles to communicate specifications and tolerances, often battling a language and cultural barrier in the process. Defining and then assuring adherence to quality standards are much more difficult across thousands of miles, multiple time zones, and vast cultural differences. Getting and then keeping this right can take considerably more time and effort than working with local sourcing.

Costs of the support functions can escalate, but not be properly attributed to the offshoring that caused them. This "cost creep" may be largely unnoticed by an offshoring company. It is possible that the true costs of production approach parity as overseas labor costs escalate, currency values shift, regulations and taxes change, and material costs swing. What appeared to be a "no brainer" years in the past may become a close call or even tilt in the favor of the United States.

Determining actual costs requires involving many parts of the business in the offshoring decision. Significant costs may have been overlooked when offshoring began. Consider some of the hidden costs. Production planning must coordinate with purchasing and establish safe lead times. Then the shop will need adequate space to store a large volume of product when it arrives en masse—another cost. Sales must provide forecasting to guide purchasing as it determines order quantities. Long lead times result in oversized orders and new orders well in advance of stock depletion—yet another cost. When transitioning to imports from domestic manufacture, Human Resources may have labor surplus matters to handle, with reductions in production hours or perhaps layoffs and severance packages. Production is likely to incur unusual costs when product does arrive, as it handles more robust packaging for the long trip and anomalies such as individually wrapped parts that demand busy work to remove the wrapping. Rejected parts become part of a nightmare, especially in large volume. It is more tempting than ever to accept bad parts since the replacements could require months to arrive. It is very likely that some of these entities are omitted when the decision is made to outsource. A company that accomplishes a thorough review of offshoring costs may be surprised to learn that the advantage is either gone or almost gone.

This book tells the brief stories of companies that have offshored manufacturing and some that have reshored. We will also describe a process that any manufacturer can use to check the real costs of offshoring—ideally, to determine if reshoring is a good idea (or to avoid making an errant offshoring decision).

A story that might surprise some people is that of Hershey chocolates. The Hershey Company essentially built the town in Pennsylvania, yet shocked everyone when it seemingly abandoned its paternalistic heritage and outsourced some candy production. The Hershey story sets the stage for this book.

REFERENCES

1. No longer made in America—Forward online global perspective from MSCI. November/December 2005.
2. Ron Scherer. A long, steep drop for American standard of living. *Christian Science Monitor,* October 19, 2011.
3. Jack Rasmus. Jobs, offshoring, and the US budget deficit. JackRasmus.com (April 24, 2011).
4. EIR Staff. Use it or lose it: Auto capacity 50% unused and going, going, gone. *Executive Intelligence Review* 33(19) May 12, 2006.
5. David Moberg. Maytag moves to Mexico. inthesetimes.com (December 29, 2004).
6. Whirlpool Corporation: Neglect pays off. http://rt.com/news/whirlpool-neglect-out-sourcing-benton-417/ (January 23, 2012).
7. Scott Pelley. Newton, Iowa: Anger in the heartland. CBS News story (November 1, 2010).
8. Jenny Strasburg. Levi's to close last U.S. plants. *San Francisco Chronicle,* September 26, 2003.
9. Austin Weber. Whirlpool centennial: From humble roots to global production power. http://www.assemblymag.com/articles/89548 (October 27, 2011).
10. Shifting production and services to foreign locations costs United States hundreds of thousands of jobs. *Manufacturing & Technology News* 11(19) October 21, 2004.

Section II

The Hershey Kisses® Story

2

Why Hershey Made the Decision to Offshore

As the twentieth century unfolded, few would have guessed that a young Mennonite man born in the rolling hills of Pennsylvania would change the name of his hometown, and indeed, the entire world of chocolate candy. Milton Hershey, born in 1857 on a farm near Derry Church, Pennsylvania, did just that. Shrugging off the limitations of his fourth grade education, and after a brief apprenticeship, the budding entrepreneur failed at his first three attempts to create his own candy company before finally succeeding in 1883 in Lancaster, Pennsylvania, with the Lancaster Caramel Company.[1]

Milton Hershey's fascination with chocolate took root at the 1893 World's Columbian Exposition in Chicago, where he discovered German chocolate-making machinery. He purchased some equipment, installed it in his Lancaster factory, and began to add chocolate candies to his offerings. By 1903 he had sold his Lancaster business, moved back to his hometown of Derry Church, and built a new chocolate plant. At that time, this was the world's largest chocolate manufacturing facility, utilizing the latest technology in mass production. The buildings covered six acres, and initial employment was 600 people. Hershey, the entrepreneur, created his own formula for milk chocolate. The Pennsylvania location afforded easy access to a huge dairy supply, a key ingredient of the new candy.[1] In 1907 he introduced one of the most famous chocolate candies: individually wrapped Hershey Kisses.

Hershey created much more than a new product for the market. He created an entire town! Perhaps it was his Mennonite upbringing that challenged him to help others. Whatever the motivation, Hershey built the town around his factory. This included homes for employees, along with community infrastructure that encompassed a public school system and recreational and cultural space. He even had the foresight to establish a charitable foundation to continue funding much of this public investment long past his own death.

Perhaps his most famous philanthropic project was the Milton S. Hershey School for orphan boys. He and his wife were unable to have children of their own, so they poured their devotion to children into organizations that benefited the youngsters. The school opened in 1909, and 9 years later Hershey endowed the school with all of his personal Hershey Chocolate Company stock![1] The successful continuation of the school seemed secure as long as people consumed Hershey's chocolate.

Hershey's sense of personal responsibility for the well-being of the entire town was most obvious during the Great Depression. He chose that time to activate his "Great Building Campaign" and provided jobs for many who needed them. Some of Hershey's largest public buildings, including a hotel, community center, theater, sports arena, and stadium, were built during a time when little else was happening. Hershey was a man who built a legacy of helping others, based on his own personal business success. The legacy lived well past Hershey's death in 1945 and into the next century. The company he founded was a bastion of security for not only the workers, but also the entire town and surrounding area. But one day the security was breached.

In 2002 the entire city of Hershey was rocked with the news that the Hershey Trust Fund Board had voted to sell the company. This was the trust fund that financed the school and was vested with Milton Hershey's stock. The motives were sound, as the board had been advised to diversify its holdings (which were completely tied up in the Hershey Company), but the news that spread focused on possible layoffs and plant closures. Nothing like this would have been possible when Milton Hershey was alive. And what might become of the Hershey-owned entities throughout the city, including a theatre, museum, and Hershey Gardens? The board had several divestment options, including buying back company stock or selling to either of two major competitors. The board tended to operate in relative secrecy, which helped to fuel rumors and speculation. Bereft of the facts and fueled by the rumors, this created a groundswell of unnecessary passion and panic in Hershey.[2] Not surprisingly, half of the city's residents were Hershey employees, and the tsunami of fear for their jobs was overwhelming. Reaction took the form of protests, rallies, and initiation of legal challenges. Even the state attorney general got into the act with an injunction to prevent the Trust from selling the company without court approval.

So, what happened? Fortunately for Hershey, nothing! Offers to buy were rejected. Life in Hershey was secure. And for the next 5 years, life in Hershey remained as it had been. But in 2007, lightning struck again.

February 2007: Breadwinning husbands had to break the news to their families. Wives whose income kept their families comfortable suddenly had lost their security blanket. Children's college educations were at risk. Car payments and home mortgages had the rugs pulled out from under them. News of layoffs at the Hershey Company, 19 E. Chocolate Avenue, Hershey, Pennsylvania, stunned the community like Pearl Harbor in 1941. The residents could not believe it. Even those who did not work directly for Hershey had worries they had not experienced before. Ever since Milton Hershey had built the town that bore his name, job security was absolute. For the first time in history, that secure foundation had cracked and, in some cases, shattered. Some people said that 1,500 jobs were lost; others contended that the number was closer to 3,000 but the number was not as important as the layoff news itself.[3] The jobs were headed to Mexico. Was it really worth it? The very foundation of the Hershey, Pennsylvania, plant—a factory that supplied the world with chocolate—seemed to be crumbling. And there was no Milton Hershey to come to the rescue!

Nothing wakes up a sleepy town faster than the threat of major job losses. A long tradition of steady employment, replete with the best paternalistic benefits available, was suddenly in jeopardy. The news line on February 15, 2007, indicated that Hershey was outsourcing North American manufacturing to Mexico and eliminating 1,500 jobs in the process. This amounted to about 10% of its North American capacity, and the decision was based largely on recent financial results. Sales were down slightly, less than a percent, but profits were down 10%. By shifting production to Mexico, Hershey anticipated absorbing a one-time cost of about $550 million, with resulting annual savings of about $180 million.[4] On paper, the production shift looked like a real winner. In town, however, it did not look as good. Like the 2002 panic, there were very few facts to accompany the news. Tempers flared, many people assumed the worst, and another round of angst was underway.

Apparently the workers were advised that there might be some jobs cut. Unfortunately, nothing was said specifically about the jobs in the Hershey, Pennsylvania, plants. Speculation was prolific and largely negative. Many workers were upset about the lack of specifics and resulting uncertainty. Local shop owners feared their livelihoods were also at risk. Lifelong residents envisioned the end of the town as they knew it. Probably everyone in town knew at least several people who were going to be impacted, including family, friends, and neighbors. Economic damage was projected to include two entire counties—far beyond the city borders.

An e-mail from a local Hershey resident sent in July commented that Milton Hershey would be rolling over in his grave over the layoff news.[5] Blame was placed on the leadership of the company, including the then CEO Dick Lenny. Interestingly, just a few months later Lenny would announce his early retirement from Hershey. High emotion stood out in the e-mail. While the author lamented that all of Hershey's production was moving overseas, the truth was that some would remain in town and a portion was moving to Mexico. Misinformation and all kinds of wild rumors tend to spread in these situations. It is impossible to keep the correct message in the news and in local conversations.

Dick Lenny became the CEO at Hershey in 2001. His primary focus was to maintain Hershey's position as the nation's largest candy maker, which was not at all the focus of the company's founder, Milton Hershey. While Hershey was concerned more with his workers' and their families' well-being, Lenny set his priorities by financial and market performance. Early in the Lenny years, the company endured a 6-week strike at two major plants. He was CEO when the near-sale by the Hershey Trust Co. occurred. And Lenny was the one who announced plant closings, accompanied by the loss of 3,000 jobs, as some production moved to Mexico. Prior to the decision to shift production, quarterly profit had plunged 96%, the company absorbed high costs to modernize production lines, and sales were flat. Lenny defined his success by profits and sales growth, not the preservation of jobs at plants in Hershey, Pennsylvania. After only 6 years, he retired from Hershey at age 55 while 3,000 people in Hershey, lost their jobs.[6]

The Great Recession of 2008 hit the confectionary business as it hit most US businesses—hard. In Hershey, management planned to consolidate some manufacturing within the plants in Hershey, with about 600 jobs at stake in the transition. Not only would this hit the town of Hershey, but also the state of Pennsylvania. The previous year, Harley-Davidson, the famous motorcycle manufacturer, eliminated 900 jobs in the state.[7] Hershey's layoff news prompted speculation of "collateral damage" to jobs in the service sector, such as local restaurants and retailers. The snowball effect was expected to gain momentum in an economy that had no other jobs to offer.

The impact of Hershey, Harley-Davidson, and no doubt some other companies soon threatened state workers. Governor Rendell stated that as many as 1,000 state workers were at high risk.[8] Even private companies that enjoyed contracts with the state for much of their work saw declines, which in turn impacted their own employees as they lost business. The trickle-down effect works negatively because the unemployed government workers would lose their purchasing power. As their families readjusted spending habits, many more local businesses would see the resulting declines. The downward spiral is sickeningly predictable. Even local banks keep a tighter lid on lending money that is critical to business expansion. The momentum becomes more and more difficult to reverse.

For Hershey, Pennsylvania, the current condition of the chocolate company is a mixed bag. A brand new 700,000 square-foot plant houses the latest in chocolate manufacturing technology. About 600 Hershey employees were kept to run it. This is said to be the largest production operation of its kind in the Hershey global empire. Far more efficient than the 108-year-old facility it replaced, it should keep Hershey in the chocolate business for years to come. It had better…Hershey invested nearly a quarter of a billion dollars in the facility.[9]

Unfortunately, for almost 500 other workers, the new plant spelled the end of their employment dreams. Their union, faced with either agreeing to the reduction in force or a potential loss of all jobs to a neighboring state, chose to cut its losses and keep production in Hershey.[10] Daughin County, in which the Hershey plant is located, has seen its unemployment rate hover just under 8% during the past 2 years. That is very close to Pennsylvania's rate and a little better than the overall US statistics. It indicates that former workers were able to find new jobs locally, moved to find work, or gave up trying altogether.

It is safe to say that Hershey, Pennsylvania, has changed forever as a result of offshoring. Closing plants or greatly reducing employment generates bottom line results at the cost of goodwill and community image. Many people connected to the company have enacted their own personal boycotts of anything Hershey and have urged others to join them. Blogs are filled with venomous comments about Hershey's treatment of its employees, and many hearken back to the "good old days" when Milton Hershey built an empire treating his employees as his family. The historic plant in downtown Hershey has been sold. While some of these outcomes may have happened anyway, one cannot escape the conclusion that offshoring jobs negatively impacted the city of Hershey. The question that boils to the surface is one asked by every worker whose job is "offshored": Was it really financially necessary, or are some people at the top just very greedy?

REFERENCES

1. History of Hershey, Pennsylvania. www.SmallTownGems.com
2. The Hershey Company. www.Answers.com
3. Daniel Victor and Barbara Miller. CLIPS: Fear of layoffs weighs upon Hershey workers, community (02/23/07). *Patriot News,* March 8, 2008.
4. Joseph Major. Hershey to cut 1,500 jobs, open Mexico facility. *International Business Times,* February 15, 2007.
5. Carol S. Another company outsourcing. http://urbanlegends.about.com/od/business/a/hershey_mexico.htm (July 12, 2007).
6. Peter Jackson. Richard Lenny to retire as Hershey CEO. *USA Today,* October 1, 2007.
7. Diana Fishlock. Businesses brace for ripple effect if Pennsylvania lays off government workers. Pennlive.com (June 27, 2010).
8. Sharon Smith. For Central Pennsylvania, the Hershey layoffs would be "a significant impact." Pennlive.com (June 2, 2010).
9. Jamie Tarabay. Original Hershey chocolate factory set to close. National Public Radio, October 6, 2010.
10. Kevin Spak. Hershey to close original factory. www.newser.com (October 6, 2010).

Section III

Devastating Trends to Our Economy and Our American Way of Life Caused by Offshoring

3

Five Other Companies That Also Offshored American Jobs

Hershey is only one example of an American manufacturer that moved operations offshore. Tragically, we believe, for our economy, too many more companies have done this as well. Most manufacturing that has moved offshore during the past several decades is invisible to the average American. We simply are unaware of where things are made and what has shifted from the United States to overseas. This chapter looks at five more companies that touch the lives of almost everyone. Some began in the United States, but moved a portion or all of their manufacturing offshore during particularly challenging economic times for them. One company never made its product in the United States. But they have this in common: They have impacted the lives and hearts of virtually every American. Consider how much more impact they could have if they employed Americans to make the products they sell here.

RADIO FLYER

Very few of us did not have a little red wagon when we were growing up. Odds are it was a Radio Flyer wagon, made by a private manufacturing company in Chicago. Started in 1917 by Antonio Pasin, this was the story of an Italian immigrant with a dream and a destination. Despite his exemplary woodworking skills, he had difficulty finding work after arriving in America and was forced to take some unskilled jobs until he could save his way into starting his own business. By 1923 his "Liberty Coaster

Company" employed several others and was on its way, building children's wooden toy wagons. The firm really took off after the 1933 World's Fair, coincidentally held in Chicago! There, Pasin borrowed heavily and created a 45 ft tall exhibit touting the "Radio Flyer" wagon.[1] The little red wagon maker never looked back.

Modeling his production after Henry Ford's automobile plant, Pasin switched from wooden wagons to steel stampings and ensuing mass production. He was able to make 1,500 wagons a day, eclipsing any dreams he had when making them from wood in a rented woodshop. This allowed him to sell wagons for $3 each, even during the Great Depression. The business employed growing numbers of workers, many of them Italian immigrants just like Pasin. Along with steady pay, they also received training in English and financial aid to build homes. Pasin was a very benevolent employer, empathizing with his immigrant employees since they reminded him of his early years in America.[1]

The product, the little red wagon, was one for the ages. Years after his death, in 2003, Pasin received a prestigious award as one of the great toy innovators, an award bestowed by the Toy Industry Hall of Fame. This came 4 years after his little red wagon had been inducted into the National Toy Hall of Fame.[2] In 2011, *Time Magazine* named the little red wagon as one of the top 100 toys of the greatest toys of all time. Antonio Pasin had hit a grand slam home run!

During the war years in the 1940s (WWII), the company switched production to gasoline and water cans, solely to aid in the war effort.[2] This established the heritage of a great American company—one that would put its own interests on hold to support a critical national event. In fact, this patriotic action alone testifies to the value of domestic manufacturing. One never knows when our very existence as a nation will rely on companies like Radio Flyer.

During the 1950s the company developed and built numerous other products, such as assorted toys and even garden equipment including wheelbarrows. It was only natural that a company successful with one product would branch out into others. Ownership and management remained in family hands, and by the 1990s Pasin's grandchildren were running the business.[1]

In 2004, there was a significant change in direction for Radio Flyer. Pasin's grandson, Robert Pasin, decided that production costs in the United States were too high, and he switched production of wagons to the world's leading toy manufacturing nation, China. At that time, China produced approximately 80% of the world's toys. Making the famous little red wagons would be only a minor blip on the Chinese manufacturing radar, but the switch was a body blow to those who lost their jobs in Chicago. Almost half of the 90 production workers saw their jobs vanish by the end of 2004.[3] Radio Flyer was now a distribution company, no longer making the famous red wagons.

Ironically, Radio Flyer has been named a top place to work for at least 5 years running. Beginning in 2009, Best Places to Work in Illinois honored Radio Flyer, despite the fact that most of its factory jobs had been outsourced. While commendable for those currently employed, it is bittersweet for the many factory workers who lost their good jobs due to an outsourcing decision.

Working in Radio Flyer's favor is the uncanny lack of awareness of most American consumers when it comes to product sourcing. Most consumers are more brand conscious than they are conscious of country of origin. Cultivating a culture of manufacturing origin awareness is a tall order and requires more marketing power and resources than most companies possess. Consequently, Radio Flyer president Robert Pasin is correct in his assessment that his brand is still Chicago.[3] Few potential customers would avoid buying a Radio Flyer wagon based on where it is made, but most would recognize the brand and make their selection based on that. One might be able to count on one hand the number of customers who have not purchased a Radio Flyer wagon since they have been made in China. If consumers only knew what impact their purchasing decisions had on the lives of others.

The other part that confounds in this situation is company size. When large companies representing thousands or even tens of thousands of workers move offshore, people notice. When one small company lays off about 50 workers to begin production overseas, the event is scarcely newsworthy. Unfortunately, Radio Flyer is one of many companies that have moved production offshore. The numbers begin to add up quickly as more and more companies shift production. Large companies in small towns create more economic chaos in the community when they offshore than small companies in large cities, such as Radio Flyer in Chicago. It may not noticeably impact the city's unemployment level, but people and their families are devastated.

LA-Z-BOY

One can scarcely say "La-Z-Boy" without adding "recliner." This famous furniture manufacturer began operations in 1928, when two cousins in Monroe, Michigan, started their business. Their business concept was wrapped around a chair, and a particularly comfortable one. Once the concept was established, they held a contest to find a company name.[4] We can all agree that the contest result was a huge success, and La-Z-Boy is now a household name.

Incorporating mechanics into the chair to make it recline was genius. For the next 40 years, they made numerous improvements and modifications to the chair. Fifty-three years after its founding, La-Z-Boy was generating $150 million in annual sales![4] Many people today might consider a recliner a necessity.

The original chair was a wood-slat design, far from the mental image most people form when thinking about the brand. The original wood-slat chair incorporated the feature that would put La-Z-Boy on the map: It reclined. Using a series of trials and errors, with the help of orange crates serving as mock-ups, the two cousins perfected the recliner. They built their first factory in the late 1920s, using a small electric motor to power the entire building. A shortage of capital and the onset of the Great Depression made finances a major challenge, but their family came through with sufficient cash to support and grow the business.[5] Surviving the trials of a start-up business and turning it into success highlight the mantra of great companies. They have good product ideas, they turn them into viable products, and they do whatever is necessary to succeed despite the trials of cash shortages and other hurdles.

Eventually the company branched off into reclining sofas, and by 1983 was offering a full line of home furnishings. Unlike most of its competitors in the furniture business, however, La-Z-Boy holds a number of patents on the mechanics most of us never see. The genius is buried beneath the comfortable cushions and attractive fabric. For many reasons, this is an American manufacturing company with a wonderful success story to share.

Unfortunately, by 2001 it began to shutter a number of its US plants, laying off thousands of workers. Following the pattern of so many other manufacturers, La-Z-Boy closed 20 plants and sent wood furniture work to China. In August of 2004, it announced the closure of four more plants and the layoffs of an additional 645 factory workers. Cities affected included

Lewisburg and White Deer, Pennsylvania; Hudson, North Carolina; and Booneville, Mississippi. Some domestic production was maintained, and the company's financials improved somewhat.

At the time, in 2004, La-Z-Boy was the second largest US furniture manufacturer. The offshoring strategy was touted as the salvation of the company, as the flood of cheaper imports was driving US furniture manufacturers to their knees.[6]

By 2008 the offshoring strategy had changed somewhat for La-Z-Boy. Then, the country of choice was Mexico. Its location bordering the United States minimized both transportation costs and shipping delivery times. Significantly diminished labor costs in Mexico appealed to company leaders as they considered the inherently labor-intensive nature of furniture manufacturing. NAFTA (North American Fair Trade Agreement) actually encouraged such corporate offshoring decisions, removing the most onerous barriers to trade within North America. But the impact on most workers losing their jobs to the foreign competition was that they would never again have wages and benefits as substantial as what they lost.

Domestic jobs continued to vanish as outsourcing kept happening. Cutting and sewing operations shifted completely to Mexico in the middle of 2008, eliminating 630 positions when a Utah factory closed. The remaining production at that facility was shifted to five existing facilities—all that was left of a one-time massive US manufacturer—adding a total of 400 jobs to those facilities.[7]

In a somewhat ironic twist, La-Z-Boy committed to build a brand new world headquarters in the company's original home town of Monroe, Michigan. The $57 million project includes a 200,000 square foot building on a 40-acre site. The good news, for Monroe at least, is that the project will add 50 new jobs and retain 450. Corporate sales in the third quarter of 2013 were almost $350 million, which indicates the relative size and strength of the company that had its very humble beginnings just 85 years ago![8]

With the abandonment of numerous plants and workers in its rear view mirror, La-Z-Boy has recently demonstrated that it can still compete with the best manufacturers. Its US plant in Dayton, Tennessee, was named an *Industry Week* best plant in 2012. Yes, this plant even produces, among many other items, the famous La-Z-Boy recliner! The key is its Lean journey, with manufacturing cells, employee incentives, and a culture of continuous improvement.[9]

Focusing on people, equipment, and processes has been vital to progress. As the workers in the Dayton plant know, reducing waste is paramount to their collective success. One wonders how successful the rest of the manufacturing base of La-Z-Boy may have been with a similar approach. It is the employing of Lean principles, engaging the workers at all levels and involving them in the business, continuously improving, and becoming increasingly productive that can successfully support domestic manufacturing for the foreseeable future.

NIKE

It is hard to think of athletic shoes and NOT think of Nike. The brand practically defines the category. A relatively new company, it did not exist until 1964. Yet, in just 32 years the company had revenues of almost $7 billion! Clearly, this was a company that did many things right.

Two people's lives intersected to form one of the most well-known brands in existence today. It is not surprising to learn that athletics was involved. In 1959 Bill Bowerman was the track coach at the University of Oregon. To help gain a competitive edge, he was always on the lookout for good, lightweight shoes for his runners. One of the track team members that year was Phil Knight, and this relentless search for better shoes stuck with him as he advanced to work on his MBA at Stanford just a few years later.[10]

One of Phil's MBA courses was a semester project to create a small business with a marketing plan. Relying on his recent past experience, he suggested a company that imported high-quality and low-cost shoes from Japan into the United States for distribution. The idea was considered intriguing, but not particularly noteworthy. One wonders how many times Phil's teacher, Frank Shallenberger, has kicked himself for not investing early in this business.[10]

Following school, Phil traveled to Japan on part of a world tour, a trip that today's youth would consider part of "finding" themselves. While in Japan, he interviewed with a Japanese running shoe manufacturer called Tiger. His idea? Sell the Japanese shoes to American runners. He made a sufficiently good impression and he was soon selling Tiger shoes. Within a year he had sold $8,000 of the shoes and was ordering more. He was working with his former track coach, Bill Bowerman, and they soon had the need to hire a full-time salesman as their business grew.

By 1971 the company was using the name Nike (the Greek goddess of victory) and the now famous trademark swoosh. The swoosh design was the brainchild of Caroline Davidson, an advertising student at Portland State University. Phil Knight was teaching accounting classes and asked Caroline to design a logo for a shoe. For a tidy sum of $35, Phil had his design and introduced it on the side of a shoe in the spring of 1972. Within 10 years sales skyrocketed from $10 million to $270 million. It is unclear whether Nike helped to spawn the fitness revolution in America or was simply the beneficiary of good product timing as the revolution began.[10] Either way, Nike's success is undisputable.

Unlike Radio Flyer and La-Z-Boy, Nike began with outsourcing the manufacture of its products. This is an example of opportunity cost, or missing jobs that never existed in the United States. Most shoes sold in this country are not made here, yet the manufacture of them employs tens of thousands of foreign workers. Consider the potential US jobs if even some of Nike's shoes were made locally. While Nike never employed Americans in shoe manufacturing, it has experienced some of the problems shared by companies that use overseas manufacturers. Nike's story includes the ingredients of what could have been (US jobs) as well as what has been (a multitude of problems encountered due primarily to making shoes overseas).

What began in Japan has spread mostly into Asia, and more than 700 different shops produce its goods. Interestingly, most of these plants are not owned by Nike. Instead, the company chooses to engage them as subcontractors, over which they have limited control. This, combined with the underlying motivation to produce the most at the lowest cost, has led to a serious public relations problem for Nike. Had Nike manufactured shoes in the United States, these problems would likely not have occurred.

The problem first surfaced in Vietnam in the late 1990s. Nike's impact on that country was significant, as it alone was responsible for 5% of the country's entire gross domestic product in 1999! Five factories, none actually owned by Nike, employed more than 35,000 people. One factory alone employed 10,000 and was considered the worst work conditions offender of the five. Routine violations of environmental regulations led to work-related illnesses among the workers. Workdays were stretched well beyond legal overtime limits, and monthly (not weekly or daily) salaries of about $40 were insufficient even in Vietnam. Add a dose of physical and verbal abuse by the managers, and the image of "sweatshop" comes to mind. The colossal impact of Nike on the country's economy may have contributed to the reluctance of the Vietnamese government to take any action. From Vietnam's perspective, the gainful employment of so many citizens would be at risk if the country balked at Nike's labor practices. Of course, Nike's response to any who complained was that it did not own any of the factories, but only purchased the goods these factories produced. Others, in fact, owned the factories.

By the late 1990s, human rights organizations had picked up the scent of the questionable labor and environmental practices and began their own public relations campaigns against Nike. Protests and informational campaigns spread throughout more than 10 countries, and Nike was forced to respond.[11]

In May 1998, Nike began to make significant changes to both environmental and labor practices. The toxic chemicals, glues, and solvents used as cleaners were replaced with environmentally friendly water-based substitutes. This dramatically reduced work-related illnesses in just 1 year. In a major policy shift, Nike also agreed to follow US workplace laws in its foreign factories. This addressed the issues of workday length, child labor, and even minimum wage. Worksites also became transparent, introducing ongoing accountability as an answer to the constant complaints of the global workers' rights groups. An added bonus was worker access to basic education. Many of the workers were young women lacking educational opportunities from any other means.[11]

Nike's resounding success in the marketplace forms a convincing argument that it has weathered the controversial firestorms of human rights violations without substantial damage to its sales. Occasional flare-ups continue, such as a 2011 report of problems in a factory in Indonesia.[12] But Nike's market domination also continues, and fiscal year 2012 revenues exceeded $24 billion. Virtually none of Nike's competitors have any manufacturing in the United States either. Based on current practices and existing wage gaps between Third World countries and the United States, bringing this industry to our shores seems unlikely anytime soon. It begs the question: Could shoes be made in the United States? Arguably, there are plenty of unemployed Americans available to make them. Even if Nike outsourced to local US manufacturers, it would still avoid the public relations problems encountered as a result of its overseas production. What we have not examined directly is the vast inventory of shoes in process and in transit at any one time. Judging by the number of shoe styles and sizes available in most stores, this number is monumental. This long supply chain carries a significant cost, even when the product is relatively inexpensive.

Supporting potential domestic shoe manufacturing is the growing consumer desire for virtually instant delivery (made much more difficult with long international supply chains) and product differentiation/customization (made challenging due to massive inventories required). Perhaps some clever engagement of automation coupled with individual consumer online design capabilities and incredibly quick delivery will lead to domestic shoe production.

LEVI STRAUSS

Blue jeans. One apparel item that remains wildly popular after years of being in style is blue denim jeans. Many people understand that these were "invented" by Levi Stauss. Strauss, an immigrant from Bavaria, started his work life with a California branch of the family dry goods business. Twenty years later, in 1873, Strauss and a tailor, Jacob Davis, received a patent for riveted work pants made from denim. The invention was the application of copper rivets to reinforce the major strain points on pants, such as pocket corners. Davis had the idea, but was short on financial resources. He joined Strauss (his supplier of material) to apply for the patent.[13] Originally intended strictly as work attire, they have become a fashion statement for many people and are worn almost anywhere and everywhere today.

The spread of blue jeans was initially slow and did not move into the East until the 1930s. Serendipitously, the US government in World War II declared jeans an "essential commodity," which contributed to their fame. In 1946 the company consisted of only two plants, 15 salespeople, and virtually no business east of the Mississippi River. During the next 30 years Levi Strauss would add almost 50 more plants, 22,000 salespeople, and have offices in 35 countries! Most of that growth occurred between 1964 and 1974 under the corporate leadership of George Simpkins Sr. During that decade he oversaw the expansion from 16 plants to 63, all in the United States. A major part of that phenomenal growth was the result of a strategic acquisition of the Great Western Garment Company, or GWG. Simpkins was known for his passionate care for the workers and utilized pay for performance in many job classifications to reward hard work. In a highly unusual move, Levi Strauss even air-conditioned some of its press plants simply for worker comfort.[14] From the Levi Strauss worker perspective, the company's zenith was in the mid-1970s.

Jeans became popular youth apparel in the 1950s and 1960s. Their popularity led to increased competition, primarily from overseas producers. Sadly, between 1981 and 1990 Levi Strauss closed 58 of its US manufacturing plants.[15] The unraveling of the US manufacture of jeans happened about as quickly as did the growth.

By 2003, there were only two remaining plants in the United States and three in Canada. Levi Strauss announced that almost 2,000 jobs would disappear as they closed these five North American plants during the ensuing 6 months. The company celebrated its 150th year in business by ending production in the United States. A small amount of work remained, but in the hands of subcontractors.[16] The year before (2002), the firm even closed the plant in San Francisco, home of its headquarters, and 100 people were suddenly looking for other employment.[17] Depending on one's point of view, the company was either slow to transfer work to low-cost labor countries and held out too long by keeping production in the United States longer than its competition, or it was a fiend for offshoring when it finally pulled the trigger. Of course, not only Levi Strauss but also the entire apparel industry was sourcing labor in Asia and Latin America. From 1997 to 2005 Levi Strauss saw 40% sales erosion at the expense of the imported competition.

One of the plants closed near the end of the exodus to offshoring was in San Antonio. The devastating reality of job loss is best expressed by the person losing the job[18]:

> In one case, Clara Flores, 54, a hem sewer in San Antonio who has been at the company for 24 years and was president of the plant's union, says that Levi's is providing retraining and other benefits. But she says it will be hard to find work with the benefits she had at Levi's: $18 an hour in wages, four weeks of annual paid vacation, and family medical and dental benefits for $24 a week. "Where are we ever going to find something like this?" she asks.

Another worker, with only 3 years of seniority, commented on the reactions of her co-workers. "There was shock and anger. A lot of people cried," said Hope Villanueva. Forty-five-year-old Maria Hernandez, with 26 years seniority, said, "We were blessed to be here. We're never going to find a place like this."[16]

The primary offshoring argument from the past was to lower costs, the result of significantly cheaper labor. Couple the ridiculously low hourly wages of under $0.25 in some countries as recently as 2002 with low or no cost of benefits, relaxed and/or unenforced labor laws, and similarly unchallenging or nonexistent environmental laws, and one has a recipe for offshoring. Now other factors are changing the equation, tilting in the favor of reshoring for some industries. Proximity to markets, manufacturing process efficiencies, dependable quality, rising costs in many Third World countries, increasing attention to environmental issues across the globe, continuous improvement cultures in manufacturing, and more are making domestic manufacturing more attractive. Unfortunately, this pattern has not yet impacted the apparel industry, still largely entrenched offshore. We await bold innovation that could tie custom sizing, potentially unique individual design, automated production, and quick delivery (perhaps even directly to customers' homes)— all predicated on domestic factories.

WHIRLPOOL®

We conclude our sampling of offshoring companies with a look at Whirlpool. Each company we have reviewed is a consumer products provider. In only one case, Nike, was production outsourced from company inception. The rest, including Whirlpool, began as US manufacturers who became highly successful and then, at some point, began offshoring work. The shifting of production was typically explained as necessary for addressing stiff competition. In each case, the human toll (in the United States) was largely ignored. The globalization argument is that the overall well-being of both producing and consuming countries is enhanced by trade. That argument neglects the human toll on those losing their jobs. Still, the consumers clearly benefit from lower costs and consequentially increased purchasing power. Globalization theoretically increases the standard of living for the majority. A vital question remains, however: Should we consider the lost jobs and industries a permanent condition, or is it possible that we can regain a competitive toehold in manufacturing?

Success from apparent failure: This was the genesis of Whirlpool. In 1908, a certain Lou Upton invested his savings in a household equipment manufacturing venture. Unfortunately, it failed before getting started, and he was faced with the option of salvaging a piece of what remained. He chose wisely! He chose to keep patents on a hand washing machine that he envisioned one day becoming electric.[19]

Lou joined forces with his Uncle Emory and brother, Fred, and together they formed the Upton Machine Company and began producing motor-driven wringer washers.[20] Most of us today have no concept of the time and energy required to launder by hand with a wringer washer, but we can appreciate that this was a major improvement for those doing the laundry for their families in 1911.

Prior to the introduction of the electric motor to washing machines by Upton, doing laundry was both time consuming and physically exhausting. It could easily take someone an entire day to do the family laundry. And the wringing needed to extract the excess water after rinsing was tedious and taxing. The introduction of electrically powered wringers as part of the washing machine brought both convenience and danger. From a pure convenience standpoint, it was wonderful because it eliminated the hand cranking. The danger was feeding laundry between two motorized opposing cylinders without unintentionally feeding body parts, particularly hands and arms. For this reason, wringers were also known as "manglers." Eventually, after more developments, the electric motor could spin the clothes dry, eliminating the need for wringing and thereby eliminating the physical dangers.[21] Upton probably had no idea of the positive impact his electric washing machine would eventually have on daily life.

The fledgling company was tested early. On its first major order for 100 machines, a gear in the transmission failed. Every machine was at risk. Displaying integrity rare in the business world and backing for its products, Upton Machine replaced the gear in every machine with a robust replacement. The customer for the 100 machines was so impressed that it doubled the size of the order.[20] This story is a testimonial to the type of people the Uptons were and how they conducted their business.

In 1917 Lou Upton again set a business precedent when he provided a paid vacation for his more senior employees. He actually sent a letter to the employees' spouses to encourage a real vacation and not simply time to accomplish some projects around the house. Factory employees in that era were unaccustomed to such benefits. The text of one letter demonstrates Upton's human touch and genuine concern for his employees[22]:

Dear Mrs. Hill,

This year we are starting a new system—which is giving our men, who have been with us a certain length of time, a vacation with pay. Bill has worked hard and with our interest always in mind and we want to start showing that we appreciate it. From Wednesday, July 25th, to Monday, July 30th, is his vacation period and we want you to work with us to see that he gets the most good out of it.

Plan some fishing trips or picnics—take the St. Joseph River boat trip, have some beach parties and so forth. Don't let Bill clean out the basement or the chicken coop or have him do odd jobs around the house; you and the family get out in the sun and the fresh air and just have a good time. We will feel amply repaid if Bill comes back with a good tan on his face as we'll know then that he has had God's open air for a good tonic.

With best regards, we remain…

Very Sincerely Yours,

Upton Machine Company
L. C. Upton

The company grew quickly through its first few decades and needed a merger to meet growing customer demand. At this point it was the Nineteen Hundred Washer Company of New York. Like most manufacturing companies in the United States during WWII, the company switched to the production of war materials needed for the military. In 1945, at the conclusion of the war, it returned to producing washers and then saw growth into other major home appliances. In 1950 the name was changed to the familiar Whirlpool Corporation.[20]

The product line expanded to include laundry, home heating, and cooling, spanning the activities of the typical American kitchen. Reflecting good corporate citizenship, in 1970 Whirlpool formed an Office for Environmental Control and applied environmental standards throughout its factories. Continued growth was bolstered by the purchase of KitchenAid in 1986 and Maytag in 2006.[22] Whirlpool grew into a virtual empire.

In 2009 the tide was turning against Whirlpool's domestic manufacturing. A decision to move refrigerator production from Evansville, Indiana, to Mexico would cost 1,100 employees their jobs. The company insisted the plant closure had nothing to do with employee performance, but rather was all about cost. Mexico offered significantly lower labor costs while preserving a supply chain that did not grow by too much distance.

This closure continued a trend of closing smaller plants as Whirlpool consolidated its production into larger plants. The company's explanation was that it had added too much capacity between 2004 and 2007.[23]

The workers, and specifically their union, the ICE-CWA, saw it differently. From their side, they saw it as the result of corporate greed and an escape from US environmental laws. Mexico offered a "better deal" on both fronts. The workers also saw the move as a direct result of NAFTA. To them, NAFTA was simply a tool to move good-paying US jobs to Mexico. Based on the experience in Evansville, that was happening.[24]

Adding fuel to the fire, Whirlpool received a $19.3 million grant from the US Department of Energy. Under the banner of taxpayer stimulus funds, this proved inflammatory as workers saw their government subsidizing the very company that was moving their jobs to Mexico. A report that Whirlpool had dodged some taxes poured even more gasoline on this public relations fire.[25]

The most recent news from Whirlpool is both encouraging and helpful. First, an August 2012 announcement promised the addition of some jobs at one of Whirlpool's Ohio plants. At least part of the increase of 120 positions was attributed to the return of manufacturing from China. About 630 full-time workers saw an additional 120 new faces joining them. This particular plant made mixers and blenders. Second, Whirlpool contends that 80% of what is sold in the United States is actually made in the United States. That is a far cry from some companies, such as Nike, who make almost nothing of what is sold in this country. Whirlpool operates five plants in Ohio, and these plants house almost half of the 22,000 US-based employees. This fact would not appease the many workers who lost their good manufacturing jobs, but it mollifies those who contend that the company has offshored all or most of its manufacturing.[26]

These five companies—Nike, Whirlpool, Levi Strauss, La-Z-Boy, and Radio Flyer—are but a small sampling of the many companies that either moved or engaged manufacturing offshore. Arguably, their impact on our culture and even the entire planet is massive. From a consumer standpoint, the results are wonderful, as the standard of living has risen and we can purchase more goods with less money. Yet, largely hidden under this positive glow is the anguish of many people who lost (or never had the opportunity for) jobs making the goods we buy. It may be unrealistic to think that everything we use should be made domestically, but we contend that much of the offshored production would benefit the companies and our country if it were domestic. The landscape is changing, offshoring's negative impact is becoming more visible, and technology advances are making local manufacture more appealing than ever before.

America is a country blessed with abundant natural resources, a favorable agricultural climate, available fresh water, and a history of manufacturing. All these and more have combined to provide the best standard of living the world has known. Manufacturing is but one piece of the success, but it is a vital piece. Our contention is that we must continue to make things if we are to continue to be great. Recognizing that cheaper labor is abundant around the globe, it may require a little bit more of good old American ingenuity to compete successfully. Since our founding, our country has been known for ingenuity and hard work. This work spirit inspires creativity and inventiveness, providing us a competitive edge. Moving production offshore simply to take advantage of cheap labor is, in our estimation, only good for the short term. A long-term strategy of making things and making constant improvements and developing new things is in our collective best interest.

A key element in the offshoring decision is accurately assessing all of the costs involved. Some seem relatively easy, such as delivered price of a given product (sometimes called "landed cost"). Tools exist to assist in cost determination, and these are particularly effective at highlighting some of the costs that may be overlooked. There are a number of costs that do not necessarily make it to the bottom line, yet they exist and have real impact. Good corporate citizens should at least be cognizant of these as they make decisions about offshoring.

REFERENCES

1. Radio Flyer. *The Play and Playground Encyclopedia.* <http://www.pgpedia.com/r/radio-flyer>
2. Radio Flyer. Wikipedia. <http://en.wikipedia.org/wiki/Radio_Flyer_(company)>
3. Little red wagon outsourced. CBS News. <http://www.cbsnews.com/2100-250_162-609517.html> (December 5, 2007).
4. La-Z-Boy. Wikipedia (http://en.wikipedia.org/wiki/La-Z-Boy).
5. La-Z-Boy incorporated history. *International Directory of Company Histories,* vol. 50. St. James Press, 2003. (http://wwwfundinguniverse.com/company-histories/la-z-boy-Incorporated-History/).
6. La-Z-Boy to lay off at least 645. *Free Republic.* http://www.freerepublic.com/focus/f-news/1188263/posts (August 9, 2004).

7. La-Z-Boy CEO explains outsourcing of US jobs to Mexico. The Turner Report. <http://rturner229.blogspot.com/2008/04/la-z-boy-ceo-explains-outsourcing-of-u.html> (April 5, 2008).

8. Jon Chavez. Construction begins on new La-Z-Boy HQ. *The Blade,* December 6, 2013.

9. Steve Minter. 2012 IW best plants winner: La-Z-Boy never rests on continuous improvement. *Industry Week,* January 17, 2013.

10. A brief history of Nike. Hincker's Homepage (<http://xro ads.virginia.edu/~class/am483_97/projects/hincker/nikhist.html>).

11. Nike in Vietnam: The Tae Kwang Vina factory (http://siteresources.worldbank.org/INTEMPOWERMENT/Resources/14826_Nike-web.pdf).

12. Nike workers "kicked, slapped and verbally abused" at factories making Converse. MailOnline. http://www.dailymail.co.uk/news/article-2014325/Nike-workers-kicked-slapped-verbally-abused-factories-making-Converse-line-Indonesia.html#ixzz2e17ro2lx (December 6, 2013).

13. Lynn Downey, Levi Strauss & Co. historian. 2005. Levi Strauss: A short biography. (http://levi.in/Downloads/PressRelease/History_Levi_Strauss_Biography.pdf).

14. Levi Strauss & Co. Wikipedia (<http://en.wikipedia.org/wiki/Levi_Strauss_%26_Co≥).

15. Outsourced. Outsaurus. <http://www.outsaurus.com/2011/08/01/outsourced-levi-strauss/> (August 1, 2011).

16. Jenny Strasburg. Levi's to close last US plants. *San Francisco Chronicle,* September 26, 2003.

17. Jenny Strasburg. Levi Strauss buttoning up its S. F. operations/Valencia Street factory to close by summer. *San Francisco Chronicle,* April 9, 2002.

18. Made in the USA? Not anymore: Levi's and Etch A Sketch are just two of the many "American" products that are now made overseas. How will the increasing outsourcing of jobs affect workers and the economy in the U.S.? The Free Library (<http://www.thefreelibrary.com/Made+in+the+USA%3f+Not+anymore%3a+Levi's+and+Etch+A+Sketch+are+just+two...-a0116138768>).

19. Whirlpool Corporation history. FundingUniverse (<http://www.fundinguniverse.com/company-histories/whirlpool-corporation-history/>).

20. Austin Weber. Whirlpool centennial: From humble roots to global production power. *Assembly Magazine,* October 27, 2011.

21. Washing machine. Wikipedia (<http://en.wikipedia.org/wiki/Washing_machine>).

22. History—Whirlpool Corporation (<http://www.whirlpoolcorp.com/100/history.aspx>).

23. Tom Murphy. Whirlpool cuts 1,100 jobs in Indiana, moving to Mexico. Manufacturing.net (August 28, 2009).

24. Dustin Ensinger. Whirlpool moving jobs to Mexico. Economy in crisis. <http://economyincrisis.org/content/whirlpool-moving-jobs-mexico> (February 22, 2010).

25. The Whirlpool spin cycle. Politics plus. <http://www.politicsplus.org/blog/2011/05/10/the-whirlpool-spin-cycle/> (May 10, 2011).

26. Thomas Gnau. Whirlpool's home appliance manufacturing brings jobs home. *Dayton Daily News,* September 1, 2012.

4

Results of Offshoring

Key to understanding the true costs of offshoring is recognizing the impact of these decisions on the offshoring companies themselves, our country, and our culture. From a somewhat myopic point of view, a company might decide its profit picture is better if it imports product. The best companies realize that their internal decisions have a widely dispersing impact even outside their corporate walls. We encourage offshoring companies to review their existing policy decisions and reconsider the overall value of importing product. We Americans all live in our culture, and we suffer as the culture suffers. What good is it if my company does well financially but harms the very culture from which my long-term customers come?

Most consumers may not realize where products are made, but they do recognize cost, quality, and delivery. Companies that have products made offshore do so for a variety of reasons, ideally focused on pleasing their customers or attracting new ones. Any company that imports products has its reasons for not manufacturing them domestically. Are offshoring decisions made with sufficient criteria in mind, or are critical pieces omitted? Do factors change over time, rendering the initial offshoring decisions invalid? Do lessons from history demonstrate that initial decisions were made without all the necessary or available data? This chapter explores the results of offshoring—results that impact the companies, their customers, and even our society.

LABOR COSTS

The most obvious reason for offshoring is cost advantage. Apparel, furniture, appliances, automobiles, shoes, and many more categories of consumer products have seen lower prices to consumers attributed to lower production costs offshore. Where labor is a large portion of the product cost, this seems to make sense. Among furniture manufacturers, one company cited the savings from health care costs as a major part of its decision to move manufacturing. Clearly, worker pay and benefits must be linked under employee compensation when analyzing cost savings and offshoring moves. From at least one vantage point, offshoring to save labor costs seems to have been good for our country: As consumers, we can buy more with less.

Perusing stores looking at labels can be very telling. In some stores, almost all products have overseas origins. One might wonder if *anything* is made in the United States! Assuming a lower price is dependent on things being made overseas, today's consumer is able to purchase much more product with the same amount of money. Looking at the number of cars, televisions, computers, cell phones, amount of clothing, size of home, etc. per household today in the United States versus a generation ago, we see a marked improvement (assuming that more is better). Some people may argue that our standard of living increased as our purchasing power increased, due in large measure to the offshoring of manufacturing.

REGULATORY BURDEN LESSENED

Other reasons for producing offshore are much less evident to consumers. These include avoiding regulatory limitations that make production more costly. For example, compliance with Environmental Protection Agency (EPA) regulations can be cumbersome and add to product cost. Whirlpool Corporation spent $30 million in compliance in one decade alone and planned for another $9 million during the next 6 years. US companies have numerous environmental rules to obey and incur costs by capturing and properly disposing of waste material and by using scrubbers or more expensive processes to limit air emissions. Some effective chemicals are banned in the United States, but readily available in other countries. Offshoring production can eliminate the additional headaches and associated costs.

Is this situation good or bad? Arguments fill both sides of this discussion. US rivers run cleaner than they have for many years, and much of this is because of EPA restrictions on what goes into our waterways. Some restrictions, it seems, make good sense environmentally.

Air pollution is another factor. Most of us know that our automobiles currently face considerably more emissions restrictions than cars of several decades ago. Gasoline formulation has changed to better protect our environment. The government has mandated increasing efficiencies for cars, to protect the environment by reducing the use of fossil fuels and by reducing the air emissions. Seemingly, these governmental oversights have been beneficial. US restrictions are much more stringent than those of many other countries around the world, including those popular offshoring destinations.

The issue is one of balance. How much restriction is prudent? And how does the rest of the world impact what the United States does or does not do? Today's travelers to cities in China or Mexico City are likely to be shocked by the amount of visible air pollution. Some of the pollution is attributable to transportation (cars, trucks, busses), and some to industry. It is obvious that the restrictions in these countries differ from our own. How much does air pollution in other countries, even those on the other side of the globe, impact our own environment? Companies that choose to produce overseas because they can pollute more without penalty need to consider the global impact of such decisions. They may make financial sense in the short term, but create negative long-term consequences for everyone. At some point, everyone on the planet shares the same atmosphere.

Balance is another matter. Organizations such as NAM (National Association of Manufacturers) argue for "balance" in creating rules and restrictions, including environmental ones. The core question is: At what price do we pollute our environment? How much pollution will we tolerate? Answers probably change over the course of time, but the discussion is unending. Perfectly clean air and water, even if attainable, are not worth the cost. Civilization as we know it would cease. We could not operate a car or truck, benefit from a power plant (coal, oil, or nuclear), or run a factory, as all of these have some negative environmental impact. We could not use tractors or combines to produce food. Our country has chosen to work through the balancing act of restrictions versus production. Similarly to setting a speed limit through a school zone (arguably, at 0 mph no children would ever be struck), there is a cost/benefit analysis. Alternate processes and chemical solutions emerge as rules are made and enforced. Nonetheless, in the short term it can be economical for producers to make things offshore where restrictions are less.

SAFETY COMPLIANCE

Worker safety is another factor driving decisions. The United States has an abundance of laws regulating the employment of people and ensuring their safety on the job. From child labor laws to 40-hour work weeks, and from MSDS (material safety data sheets) to lift truck training, companies must comply with long lists of activities and rules focused on the protection of their workers.

Disparate wages and benefits aside, freedom from the many rules and their associated costs can make offshoring very appealing. And while it may be possible to fly "under the radar" in terms of public view, more than one company has faced scrutiny for perceived employee abuse in other countries. Shoe and apparel manufacturers have been accused of exposing their workers to dangerous chemicals, using child laborers, making people work extremely long hours, and imposing questionable conditions on employees. In one case, a California wafer manufacturer was exposing its workers to high levels of arsenic. Apparently, it was easier to move production to China than to correct or improve the process. Once highlighted, such problems need immediate and transparent correction. It is easy to see how the undetected company has an economic advantage.

UNION STRENGTH

Another perceived cost savings for a manufacturer can be the absence of a difficult union. By definition, these organizations exist to better the workplace conditions for the worker. Even though the numbers of private workers in unions in the United States have been declining in recent years, an entrenched union can add cost to production. This may come in the form of work rules or contractual stipulations that interfere with productivity. Time spent on negotiations and other employee matters is an additional cost. Much or all of this goes away when a company offshores its work. With no specific accountability to either a union or to the US government, manufacturers can become unscrupulous employers or allow the distant entity to become unscrupulous. Every step away from the regulation of a union workplace can turn into cost savings.

Cost savings identified thus far include labor costs and freedom from most or all environmental regulations, wage and hour restrictions, and union contracts. Depending on the company, its processes, and the offshoring destination, these savings can be significant. But the additional costs incurred by offshoring are significant, too. These may be harder to quantify, but warrant the exercise to avoid making a bad decision:

1. Loss of control. Anyone involved in manufacturing for almost any length of time realizes that being distant from the point of manufacture is difficult. The loss of control, by itself, is at the least frustrating and, more likely, disruptive. The ingredients of a great product become almost invisible even to the insiders when the production is offshore and separated from company management. Oversight of raw materials, including quality and delivery, is left to the production component, which may be prone to compromises or to overstocking when faced with challenges of outages due to out-of-spec material or due to poor delivery.

   Bayard Winthrop founded American Giant in 2012, determined to dispel the myth that clothing cannot be profitably made in the United States. Making his now-famous hooded sweatshirt ("hoodie") originally began with material from a mill in India. Quality and logistics problems motivated a switch to nearby mills in South Carolina: Carolina Cotton Works and Parkdale. The problems of lengthy time to specify materials, overcoming the variances between lot productions, communicating effectively with the overseas producer, and simply receiving what he ordered disappeared.[1] In the end, Winthrop saved by controlling his sourcing and material quality.

2. Even more costly is the potential loss of product innovation. Being distant from the product and production processes greatly lessens the opportunity for improvement of either. Leading companies today recognize the power of improvement teams when composed of people from many different roles, also called cross-functional teams. When engineering joins purchasing, production, marketing, and even a wild card (finance? receptionist?), results are both surprising and transformational. Distant operations prevent such teams from forming and working together. It is easy to forget about a process that might benefit from improvement. It is easy to let a product linger

in the market, unchanged for too long. Languishing in either area is costly.

3. New product development suffers when management is separate from production. Development of new products is enhanced by the collaboration of many areas, and it suffers when key members of the team are apart. People involved in actually making products are tremendous idea generators, and offshoring breaks the connection between these people and those who can turn their ideas into new products. Generating or capturing product improvement ideas falls victim to the "out of sight, out of mind" phenomenon. This lost opportunity cost may be impossible to calculate, but it really matters.

4. Separation of engineering from production handicaps both engineering and production. The missing piece for both entities is feedback. For engineering, feedback on designs is vital to continuous improvement. Close contact between the two enables engineers to learn from those who use their designs. Engineering in a vacuum leads to production problems, and the absence of a feedback mechanism allows the same mistakes and design flaws to be repeated. Production problems are costly, but repeated production problems are both costly and unnecessary. From the other side, engineering frequently needs to see that new designs are properly developed in production. Following a new design through the shop enables engineering to train workers on proper fabrication and assembly. This can be engineering's opportunity to instruct. Great new product ideas may be hampered by the lack of follow-through in production.

5. Product quality can be challenging to control when the factory and office are connected. When they are a country or more apart, quality control can become an insurmountable challenge. An industrial wheel manufacturer learned this the hard way when a customer had a problem with wheel treads. The offshore producer had changed materials, without permission from the home office. The new material was deficient and caused a problem at a customer's facility. In-house quality control would have easily prevented this problem. What is the cost of a dissatisfied or disappointed customer? Consider how many customers may silently vote with their feet when time to place the next order.

6. Communication is critical in any operation. Even with the currently available technology, including Skype, problems abound when communication is not face to face. Manufacturers recognize the perils of inadequate communication as production and office struggle to meet customer orders as specified. Engineering changes are not always implemented correctly in production. These communication gaps magnify when production and management are separated by countries. Throw in a few time zone differences, a cultural barrier, and perhaps even language differences, and the gap is cavernous. Many companies attempt to mitigate these problems with periodic management visits to the production facilities. These help, but provide only sporadic communication and come at a high cost. Also, the communication is limited to the one or few who travel. Most of the management team, including salespeople, may never meet anyone in production. Impaired communication within any company makes success even more of an uphill battle. Communication problems show up as costs from delayed shipments, rework, and maybe even some lost customers.

7. For many companies, intellectual property is vital to their success. Product innovations are frequently protected with patents. Keeping sensitive information secret safeguards a particular brand. Certain processes often determine the end product, such as curing times and conditions for certain chemical processes. A company's survival may be at stake if a competitor learns of and copies any of this. When production moves offshore, the new host country and culture are often not sharing the same ethics as the United States, and internal company information is at risk. Some countries, notably China, are known for copying American products and selling them at greatly reduced prices. While this is certainly a possibility domestically even when applying the utmost caution, producing offshore can almost encourage the loss of secrecy. Recently, a survey revealed that a quarter of US companies manufacturing in China had seen some compromise to confidential information. While China disputed the report and perhaps the actual number of companies hurt may be in doubt, the fact that it is a problem is not in dispute. This cost can range all the way to the top value of the company.

8. Ask almost any company leader to identify his or her company's most valuable asset, and the overwhelming response will be "our people." Yet, when a company moves production offshore, it sheds a

large number of those people (theoretically to reduce costs). As those people leave the company, they depart with a considerable amount of talent. That potential for innovation and problem solving is lost to the company. Successful companies today garner the energy and talent from their entire team, and apply it across the entire spectrum of company operations. Cross-functional improvement teams are, by definition, engaging the raw talent and innovation of workers with varied job responsibilities and expertise to make improvements in unfamiliar parts of the company. Removing a major portion of the team, such as production, hurts not only innovation and process improvement in that realm, but also in the office. There can be a high cost to lost talent, idea generation, ingenuity, and problem-solving capability.

9. Offshoring production almost always results in more inventory. This is due to distant suppliers and the resulting longer lead times. Ordering and receiving material from overseas takes months and requires much higher inventory levels to meet customer demand. Increasingly, even in the world of B2B (business-to-business), customers are unwilling to wait for their orders. Quicker delivery often trumps lower prices. Mitigating the longer delivery means much higher levels of inventory, particularly when demand is spotty or spikes. This takes both space and cash, and there is a cost associated with both of these. Also, managing higher levels of inventory presents challenges. First, any items that have a limited shelf life need very accurate date tracking and potentially risk scrapping due to spoilage. Second, simply keeping track of the items may challenge some systems, and product is known either to vanish or to get damaged when it sits around. Third, items that are seasonal or that see design changes periodically may become obsolete while they wait to be sold. Few see the value of inventory that simply exists for long periods of time. Seldom is having excessive inventory an advantage. More often, it comes at a high cost.

10. Tying up lots of cash on product either in the supply chain or in storage prevents better use of that cash. It is not unusual for a company to pay up front for goods purchased offshore as early as the placement of an order. Considering production and transit time, this could easily stretch into months. Then, selling a larger inventory takes time, meaning considerable cash may be tied up in the selling process for long periods of time. Smaller companies may not be able to handle

such costs, and even those on good financial footing may not want to live with constrictions that might impact other business opportunities. American Giant's Bayard Winthrop found this to be a major factor in his emerging sweatshirt business. "Overseas apparel manufacturing also means paying well in advance for shipments that will then sit on a boat for a month before ever reaching US shores, which ties up cash. Arrangements with US manufacturers tend to be more flexible," he says. "The result is less upfront risk."[2] There is an opportunity cost connected to having inventory. The more cash is tied up in inventory, the less that is available to run the business or to invest in improvements.

11. Once goods arrive from an offshore producer, costs may surface that are either hidden or simply omitted in calculating the true cost. It is possible for goods to be handled more than twice (putting into storage and then taking out), and every handling episode increases the cost as well as the risk of damage or loss. Goods may become damaged by improper handling or by the passage of too much time (rust or decay). If product arrives either defective or damaged in transit, it may lead to rework, which is always costly. Returning product for any reason is frequently untenable due to transit times and required inventory levels. Sending everything back to the overseas supplier may leave a company without product to sell. Should rework costs be covered by the supplier, there is still the scheduling challenge of building unexpected time requirements into a schedule. When this rework occurs on a large scale, it is likely that key people in management are aware and can track the costs. When it is on a smaller scale, it is easy for the costs to go unreported and unnoticed. It is probably rare that an importing company does not incur unanticipated costs over the course of time. These must be built into the product cost or they will diminish the company's earnings.

Nationally, the offshoring pros and cons are somewhat different. From the consumer's viewpoint, less expensive goods are welcome. Sam Walton transformed American retail when he started his Wal-Mart chain, and its success has been predicated on low prices for a massive variety of consumer items. People can buy either more goods or larger sizes than they might otherwise purchase (televisions, for example). This phenomenon of increased purchasing power effectively raises the standard of living. Still, there have been some adverse side effects, too.

When plants close, dozens, perhaps hundreds, and sometimes even thousands of jobs may be lost almost instantly. An offshoring decision that results in one or more plant closings in the United States leads to job losses and disruption that relatively few appreciate. Sure, we all enjoy the lower prices when we go to the store, but we need to think about some of the higher costs we incur, too.

Job loss leads initially to unemployment and, normally, unemployment compensation. Unemployment compensation comes from taxes, and eventually those taxes find their way into product prices. Sustained unemployment can result in more demand on welfare and food stamps and other support organizations that exist to help people in this situation. Again, government programs depend on taxes and, at some level, those additional taxes find their way to taxpayers. Consumers see higher prices, but most do not "connect" the cause (job loss due to offshoring) to the effect (higher taxes or less of other government services). Some people might argue that this is covered by the ever increasing national debt, at least at the federal level, but that is hardly good news.

Piggybacking on unemployment is the resulting loss of tax revenue. Those who lose their jobs are suddenly no longer paying taxes, so every government entity from a city or county through the IRS sees a corresponding drop in revenue. In cities where budgets must be balanced, a big enough revenue decrease can impact the jobs of some city workers, including fire and police. The domino effect ensues. At the federal level, the national debt climbs.

New trends are emerging as the Great Recession impacts our economy long after it has officially ended. One is the erosion of skills, at least in manufacturing. Young people in school looking ahead toward possible careers notice unemployed relatives and friends who had been working in manufacturing, and they develop other career pathways. Interest in manufacturing careers drops, and the supply of qualified next-generation workers shrinks. Certain skills, such as tool and die makers and machinists, are currently in short supply in many areas. People are reluctant to invest time and money in training (or retraining) when there is little confidence that the training will lead to jobs. It can take years to turn such a trend around.

Another trend is systemic unemployment and a growing number of people dependent on government assistance. The welfare stigma is being replaced by an acceptance of welfare as a normal state for many people. Free rides over a long period of time become expected, or the norm. Many parents are realizing this phenomenon as their adult children move home and depend on mom and dad for support. Absent some strong motivation to make a change, the "good life" is hard to leave. A new mentality and attitude develop, and the idea of going back to work starts to fade. Opinions vary widely on how long and how much unemployment compensation and welfare benefits should be. But most people can agree that being employed is a better option than relying on government assistance. It is in our collective best interest to minimize the long-term adjustment to the "welfare state."

When enough of an industry moves offshore, it becomes much more difficult to reestablish that industry; both supply chain and expertise are impacted. One example (of many) is the manufacture of industrial pneumatic tires—not those we use on automobiles, but rather those on factory equipment. Many common sizes of these tires are now exclusively produced overseas. No domestic manufacturers remain. One wonders if the United States could produce them if necessary. Many observers consider the national security implications of the loss of manufacturing capability to be daunting.

This completes our list of the costs of offshoring. We do not claim that this offshoring cost list is exhaustive, but it is considerably more comprehensive than lists we suspect were used for many offshoring decisions. Innovation almost naturally springs out of the process of making things. Ideas emerge for improvements, and prudent management encourages experimentation. Engineering works in concert with production, and ideas can be proven or disproven. A study conducted to provide real data on this topic actually found that offshoring firms saw an advantage in the area of innovation, but the study omitted firms that outsourced all their production.[3]

A critical facet is that of opportunity costs. That is, a firm that offshores some production may continue to innovate, but how much innovation is lost by offshoring that could have been realized had the offshoring not occurred? One wonders what could have been.

Another study suggests that the reason for more innovation may lie with more dollars spent on the innovation, dollars freed up from the lower costs of offshore production.[4]

Even in the world of IT (information technology), where one might suppose innovation can come independently of manufacturing, doubt abounds. The story of Kodak and camera development suggests that this once mighty company sacrificed significantly on the altar of offshoring[5]:

The troubling thing that our research turned up is that off-shoring can lead to damage to what we call the industrial commons—a set of capabilities embodied in your supplier network, your workforce, the educational infrastructure associated with a technology area. For example, in the 1960s Kodak (EK) gave up making sophisticated film cameras, and the US consumer electronics companies off-shored their product manufacturing and development. So the industrial commons for consumer electronic and optoelectronic devices in the US withered away. So when the digital camera revolution came along—even though Kodak invented the first digital camera in the 1970s—there was no longer any capability base in the US to develop or manufacture such products.

Many of the offshoring costs are extremely difficult to quantify. Some are societal costs and do not directly impact the offshoring company. They are costs, though, and some of them have serious future implications for our culture and our country. Great companies will maintain a worldview that includes their own impact on their environment—not only the physical environment, but also the societal.

Disregarding any societal costs, the direct costs to an offshoring company may be easy to overlook or ignore, but they have impact nonetheless. Many of the categories described previously may have been omitted in considering the costs of offshoring. We strongly suggest these can make a huge difference in long-term corporate success. Even the most obvious costs are changing. In fact, as the world situation changes, including costs of labor and energy/shipping costs, the financial "answer" may change as well. Offshoring companies would be well advised to "check their numbers" again to determine if the equation has changed for them. The next chapter tells the stories of some companies that reconsidered their offshoring and determined that the numbers argued for reshoring.

REFERENCES

1. Stephanie Clifford. US textile plants return, with floors largely empty of people. *New York Times,* September 19, 2013.
2. Marcus Wohlsen. How the Internet is bankrolling the world's best hoodies—And rebooting US manufacturing. <http://www.wired.com/business/2013/04/how-the-internet-makes-the-worlds-best-hoodie-possible-and-saves-u-s-manufacturing/#slideid-79083> (April 15, 2013).

3. Bernhard Dachs, Bernd Ebersberger, Steffen Kinkel, and Oliver Som. Does off-shoring hurt domestic innovation activities? VOX http://www.voxeu.org/article/offshoring-firms-innovate-more-evidence-european-manufacturers (September 7, 2013).

4. The Offshore Group. Off-shoring and innovation. http://offshoregroup.com/2013/09/05/offshoring-and-innovation/ (September 5, 2013).

5. Stephanie Overby. IT outsourcing: How off-shoring can kill innovation. CIO. http://www.cio.com/article/686597/IT_Outsourcing_How_Offshoring_Can_Kill_Innovation?page=1&taxonomyId=3195 (July 22, 2013).

Section IV

The Reshoring Trend

5

Five Companies That Brought American Jobs Back Home

Some companies have already begun the reshoring process. They have restored production to the United States after some experience with offshoring. As with many things in life, the reasons are not always simple. Many things change over time, including the market, delivery expectations, quality demands, shipping costs, currency exchange rates, and labor rates. Some companies have learned that offshored production causes more internal headaches than they anticipated, and some have seen hidden costs become obvious. For example, ET Water Systems, a small California company that manufactures irrigation equipment, offshored its production as part of the groundswell of companies moving production for lower costs. In only 5 years it learned that money tied up in lengthy shipment was costly, innovation and quality suffered from the disconnect between production and engineering, and total costs approached those of producing domestically. This chapter examines five companies that have tasted the offshoring Kool-Aid and have decided to bring production back to the United States

CATERPILLAR

A 2010 announcement of a $120 million new plant construction in Victoria, Texas, warmed the hearts of many Texans and reshoring fans in general. Potential new employment was 500 jobs! Interestingly, this was not moving production from China, where one might guess, but rather from Japan. Nonetheless, Caterpillar determined that hydraulic excavators being sold in the United States could be competitively manufactured domestically. A similar plant in China, making the same type of equipment, was planned to continue production for that market. In fact, plans included increasing production at that plant to meet the growing local demands.[1] Considering the size and complexity of Caterpillar products, it makes sense even to outsiders that production best occurs near the intended market.

Caterpillar is recognized around the world by its products' yellow color. It all started in California just after the turn of the century when steam tractors were so heavy that they tended to sink into the soft earth. Many people sought solutions, but Benjamin Holt came up with the best answer. He developed a track system to replace individual wheels, which proved to be effective in many applications. Holt's initial test of a prototype occurred in November 1904, and 3 years later he had a patent on his design. Allegedly based on a comment made by an observer of the strange-looking contraption, who noted that the device moved like a caterpillar, the name stuck. By 1910, Caterpillar was a trademarked name. Also that year, Holt opened his first manufacturing plant in the Midwest in East Peoria, Illinois, where he purchased an empty building and began operations with 12 employees. With two plants, one in Stockton, California, and the other in East Peoria, Holt was able to supply a burgeoning appetite for the innovative product. In just 2 years his company employed 625 workers.[2] The Holt Caterpillar Company was on its way.

By the time World War I started, Holt had exported more than 1,200 tractors to Europe and Russia. Intended for agricultural use, the tractors proved useful for transporting equipment in the war effort. It was the British who developed the tank we know today, and that has had huge impact on the conduct of warfare ever since.[2]

Meanwhile, in 1910 the C. L. Best Gas Tractor Company began operations and became Holt's biggest competitor. While Holt focused most of his company's efforts on military customers, Best directed his company at the growing agricultural market. The end of the war proved challenging for both companies, as the military market plunged abruptly and the nation's economy also tanked. Survival demanded that both Best and Caterpillar take on considerable debt. The companies were bitter rivals, with skirmishes typically held in the US court system, and they collectively spent more than $1.5 million attacking each other. Before the financial problems of either competitor were resolved, and before the seemingly endless court battles were settled, Holt passed away in 1920 after a brief illness.[2]

In 1925, a brokerage house suggested that the two heavy equipment manufacturing Goliaths should merge. Ironically, while Best Tractor was financially stronger, the name "Caterpillar" emerged from the joining and Clarence Best (from whom the C. L. Best Gas Tractor Company name was taken) was the first CEO. Almost immediately following the merger, sales improved and the company grew even through the Great Depression.[2]

Caterpillar is almost synonymous with infrastructure. "Cats" have been used in major building projects around the United States, including the famous Hoover Dam and Grand Coulee Dam, the Chesapeake & Delaware Canal, the Alaskan Highway, and even the Canol Oil Pipeline in the Arctic. As it did in World War I, Caterpillar assisted greatly in war support during World War II by providing more than 51,000 vehicles. Following the war, Caterpillar equipment aided in the construction of the interstate highway system initiated by President Eisenhower. By the 1950s its equipment was in use in Canada, Sweden, Uganda, Antarctica, India, Venezuela—on virtually every continent.[3]

The massive company has continued to grow, and has spread across the globe. A review of its recent employment history shows remarkable expansion with a few rough patches and some interesting shifting of jobs. During the 1990s Caterpillar restructured and reduced 20,000 union jobs in its Peoria, Illinois, headquarters, while increasing the total employment outside the United States. That rearrangement reflected the struggles it had in its unionized manufacturing plants and the movement of production to minimize the impact of disruptions. In 1992, the United Auto Workers (UAW) held a 5-month strike at two plants in Illinois. Only 2 years later, nearly 10,000 workers struck Caterpillar nationwide for 17 months. There were numerous local problems and work stoppages between the two major strikes. These disruptions in production caused delays in research and development, as it was "all hands on deck" for the remaining salaried people during the strikes. During the following decade, the Great Recession, which began in 2008, led to a loss of almost 18,000 employees. A recent tally of Caterpillar manufacturing plants shows that only 51 of 110 plants are located in the United States. Employment worldwide in 2013 was 122,400 jobs, more than half of which were located offshore.[2]

Depending on who is telling the story, Caterpillar moved production in two distinct directions as a result of labor unrest. One direction was to move work to plants in right-to-work states, traditionally in the nation's Southeast. Typically, these plants were smaller and more focused on a particular product, whereas traditional Caterpillar plants made a variety of products. The other direction was that Caterpillar outsourced work that had been, up to that point, functions performed by its own workers.[2] Labor problems continued. As recently as 2012, 780 International Association of Machinists and Aerospace Workers (IAMAW) struck for more than 3 months at the Joliet, Illinois, plant. Final agreements included a 6-month wage freeze.[4] The outcome seemed to indicate that the geographic spread of the work throughout the world and using smaller plants led to a weakening of the union's power.

This leads us to the most current events in Caterpillar's reshoring journey. As market conditions change, Caterpillar is experiencing increasing demand in North America and Europe. Thus, manufacturing in the United States makes more logistic sense than continuing to manufacture in Japan. Operating plants in the South and Southeast also follows a pattern of employment in right-to-work states, reducing the contentious labor issues Caterpillar has faced in the past.

The Texas announcement was for a new plant, not an expansion of an existing one. Since that time there have been announcements of expansion projects in Decatur and East Peoria, both in Illinois (not a right-to-work state). The two expansions were estimated at $640 million in investment capital and collectively would add 300 new jobs. Interestingly, much of the production from the additional Illinois capacity is to be exported.[5] The union will benefit from producing for the export market. Clearly, Caterpillar is not completely avoiding the union issue as it increases domestic production.

Caterpillar also announced in late 2011 news of a new 850,000 square-foot facility in North Carolina on the verge of opening. Equipped to produce axle assemblies, this plant would support the expanded production from the Illinois plants.[5] Finally, even as Caterpillar adds to US capacity, it continues to support international markets with local capacity when needed. For example, a new mining truck facility will be built in Indonesia to support Asian market demand.

Most recently, Caterpillar has experienced a significant decline in demand in 2013. The economic rebound from the recession of 2008–2009 led to expansion plans and hiring, literally around the world, for the giant equipment producer. Then, a slump in 2013 brought the expansion to a screeching halt, including trimming 13,000 jobs.[6] Sadly for the Decatur, Illinois, plant, the impact was 760 jobs.[7] Of little consolation to Decatur was previous news in early 2013 that 1,400 jobs in a Belgian plant would be cut.[8] Layoff patterns indicate that area market demand is the most significant factor in determining where Caterpillar cuts costs. Apparently, the union issues no longer dominate the strategic location plans.

It is encouraging to see this industrial giant bringing some manufacturing jobs back to the United States, particularly when the products are then exported. As an international company, Caterpillar must be very sensitive to press all over the world, particularly in countries where local plants are trimmed or closed. All recent indications point to Caterpillar's recognition that US production costs are competitive internationally.

MASTER LOCK

When most people think of a padlock, Master Lock comes to mind. Inventor and entrepreneur Harry Soref founded Master Lock in 1921 after trying to sell his invention of a lock constructed with laminated layers. The lamination was the key to the strength of his design. Existing companies were not interested, so Soref formed his own company and began with himself and five other employees. He was able to patent his innovative design in 1924, and his company continued to grow under his leadership until his death in 1957.[9] His renown as one of America's great lock experts was solidified when Harry Houdini needed Soref's help to escape from a particularly difficult set of handcuffs.[10] After Soref's death, one of the original investors in Master Lock assumed control until 1964, and the company was then sold by the Soref family heirs. It is currently owned by Fortune Brands Home and Security and is based in Milwaukee, Wisconsin.[9]

Many people know the brand by a 1973 Super Bowl ad. In that ad, a Master Lock absorbed a bullet from a sharpshooter and still functioned. It proved to be a brilliant advertising move despite consuming nearly the entire annual marketing budget. The image it created was virtually timeless and proved to be an effective advertising image for many years beyond the original 1973 sharpshooter ad.[9]

The company grew, and by 1990 it employed 1,300 workers, all in the Milwaukee area. In 1993, though, it began to offshore many of the manufacturing jobs to China and Mexico. Master Lock maintained its Milwaukee plant and used automation extensively in the production it kept. Yet the attractiveness of lower wages enticed it to move the more manual operations to the lower cost countries. Leadership claimed the offshoring move was forced by the flood of cheap imitation locks inundating the US market.[10] That reality blanketed much of the consumer market, leading many other manufacturers of other products to make similar moves.

By 2011, the landscape had changed. China was no longer the darling of US manufacturers. While China's attractiveness began with a tsunami of virtually no-cost laborers from a country with a population exceeding 1 billion, those workers became more vocal and demanded pay increases as they saw opportunity for participating in a rising standard of living. Also, the currency exchange rate, which had been held firm by Beijing as it heavily favored its own economy, began to shift under pressure from the United States and others. This movement greatly helped US exports by making them less expensive in China and made Chinese products more expensive in the United States. Finally, shipping costs quadrupled during 1 year, due in large measure to the cost of energy added to the cost of transporting product from China. While we might cheer for a round of "it is the right thing to do for America" as a fourth reason, that seldom resonates within publicly held companies. They, in fact, are normally the first to offshore and among the last to reshore due to the pressure they face from shareholders for quick positive financial results. Patriotism seems a negligible motivator.

For Master Lock, reshoring began with about three dozen workers hired to bring the Milwaukee factory population to 379. To workers returning to the plant floor, everything looked and ran much differently. Automation now dominated the production area, and a single worker might oversee several machines. The equipment produced quality parts, maintaining very tight dimensional tolerances. It also produced parts quickly, as the system pumped out a new combination lock every 2½ seconds.[10]

Labor-intensive work for Master Lock took place in Mexico, where it had established a production beachhead during the same decades it moved work to China. Some production remained in China, although that was intended for the local Chinese market and not that of the United States Perhaps unusual for a reshoring story, Master Lock received no concessions from its union in Milwaukee, nor did it receive any incentives from any governmental agencies to bring the jobs back.[10] The economic motivation was purely from market factors. The three dozen new workers eventually grew to more than 100, all reflecting the transfer of work from China to the United States. While 100 returning jobs is only a tiny blip on the national employment numbers, it is a blip in the positive direction and is a sign of a trend that can collect steam as the market conditions encourage even more reshoring.

As the jobs returned to Master Lock's Milwaukee factory, the worker profile changed markedly from the early 1990s. The low-skilled positions no longer existed. Now, workers needed skill to operate the high-tech equipment and automation that made US production economically attractive.[11] This meant at least two things for US workers. First, they would need additional skills to compete successfully for manufacturing jobs. Traditionally, these jobs pay more than those in the service sector and can be financially rewarding for those with the requisite skills. Second, the volume of manufacturing jobs has shrunk as a percentage of goods produced. Simply put, it takes fewer workers to produce a larger amount of goods. The highly automated equipment makes many more parts, and fewer workers are required. Thus, no one should expect that even a complete reshoring movement would result in the same number of factory jobs that existed prior to the massive exodus to China.

Celebrating the reshoring for Master Lock included a visit from President Obama in January, 2012.[12] His administration has heavily promoted job creation, and the Master Lock story was simply too good to pass up. Regardless of one's political bent, highlighting a manufacturing employment success was a great rallying point for all of US manufacturing and for reshoring in particular.

NEUTEX

Certainly not a household name and unfamiliar to most people, Neutex is a young company that has lived through offshoring and reshoring in a relatively short time. Founded in 1987 as a logging and construction company, the manufacturer now makes LED lighting and other environmentally friendly lighting products and began its corporate life in Houston, Texas. LED lighting, relatively new to most consumers, brings an astounding 50,000 hour life to the average bulb versus a comparatively paltry 1,200 hours for an incandescent equivalent. The LED life span even eclipses the compact fluorescent bulbs, which may last 10,000 hours. Sustainability is a huge selling point for LED lighting. Disposal is environmentally safe and does not pose the sustainability challenges that the popular fluorescent lights do.[13]

Lighting manufacturing took root in 2006 and began in Houston at company headquarters. Shortly thereafter, CEO John Higgins moved its manufacturing to China for all the typical offshoring reasons. Neutex focused mostly on price. The erroneous assumption was that a lower labor cost from China was automatically a good deal for the company when selling in the United States.[14] Had it been solely the China price, Neutex would still be producing goods in China and shipping them to the United States.

Life is seldom simple, and the offshoring experience is likewise anything but simple. Neutex may not have encountered all the problems that offshoring can bring, but it certainly had some of them. For example, Higgins found that worker productivity in China was abysmal, roughly one-quarter that of the United States.[14] When he factored in some robotic help, American productivity looked even more favorable. The anticipated labor cost advantage was not proving realistic.

The local wage base was also changing during the few years Neutex manufactured in China. That country is experiencing a rapidly emerging middle class, and consequently wages are rising quickly. By early 2012, the Chinese worker was being paid $400 a month, quite a bit more than only a few years before.[14] During the frequent trips to China to check on his production, Higgins observed the growing middle class and anticipated continued expansion of that along with accompanying wage growth. The China wage trend was definitely tilting the offshoring advantage in the favor of reshoring. When coupled with the US wage stagnation brought on by the Great Recession, the labor cost gap was narrowing rapidly.

Other significant factors emerged during the Neutex China years. One such factor was quality. Defect rates ranged as high as 55%, and product consistency was also problematic.[15] Defects in a local factory, one located near management, can be addressed immediately. When proper processes exist, any defects will be caught quickly, the problem identified, and the fix applied. In a typical Lean manufacturing operation, defects are rare, and the number of defects created per "hiccup" is very small. When large batches of product arrive from offshore, the number of defects can be huge since they likely will not be detected until arrival in the United States. In fact, it is possible that the next batch of product may be in process even while the problems from the previous production run are being uncovered! A defect-causing process could be impacting more than one large batch of product.

Assigning a real cost to defects can be difficult. Management time, including engineering or quality control inspection, proper communications, management decisions on fixes, and time or opportunity lost due to restricted sales, adds up quickly. In many cases, when the product is of relatively low value, defective product may be scrapped. If not scrapped, management may direct the local plant to salvage what product it can. This rework should be measured, as well as any additional parts or materials required. Also, in some cases, bad product may be inadvertently sold, blemishing the company's reputation and impairing future sales. Fortunately, Neutex was noticing all of this and counting the cost.

Travel to and from the offshored source consumed substantial time and money. In this case, Higgins himself made as many as five trips a year to China.[15] He also recognized that Neutex had to pay in advance for product that could take 2 months or longer to arrive in the United States. Higgins could not ignore the cost of his money idling. He considered these costs when deciding to reshore.

A cost of importing that receives little fanfare is that of shipping problems. Neutex experienced unplanned delays when its shipments were preempted by larger customers with more clout and also found itself occasionally charged for unplanned searches for contraband.[16] When product is needed, delays can be devastating. Unexpected fees and other charges must be absorbed or selling prices adjusted. Adding up all the offshoring-associated costs, Higgins decided that reshoring was in Neutex's best interest.

Once Higgins decided to reshore, he had to consider the lure of incentives from states and localities in determining where to locate production. Neutex headquarters was in Houston, but that did not necessarily mean the lighting plant had to be there, too. Interestingly, the city of Houston and the state of Texas offered no incentives to locate in Houston. Pennsylvania, Michigan, and Georgia tried to lure the business to their respective states, and other cities in Texas also made attractive offers.[17] Even so, when Higgins considered the advantages of colocation with management and the infrastructure advantages offered by Houston, it made sense to turn down incentive money from others.

Reshoring involves staffing, and depending on the worker skills required, this can be one of the more challenging components. Early in the reshoring process, Higgins worked with the IBEW (International Brotherhood of Electrical Workers) to provide staffing for the plant.[18] Undaunted by the conventional wisdom of avoiding union shops, he chose to begin with a union shop of IBEW workers. While employment projections called for eventually 250 to 300 workers in the plant, Higgins projected that numbers would reach 150 within the first 12 months. Wages started between $10 and $18 an hour, and employees would receive health insurance, perhaps the most coveted benefit of all.[14] Thinking of the local community as well as the US employment situation, Neutex reached out to military veterans with job offers, specifically targeting those disabled from battle injuries. The company even designed the workplace to accommodate these workers.

Neutex is both an interesting and an appropriate subject to study. First, it is a relatively small company. Offshoring is difficult for larger companies with sizable staffs and deeper pockets; it is even harder for smaller companies. It is very expensive in terms of travel, language barriers, cultural differences, administrative details, and logistics. Offshoring costs are generally much higher than they appear at first blush, when the lure of lower labor costs attracts.

Second, Neutex offshored just as the Chinese labor rates were beginning to increase. Higgins very astutely noticed the emerging middle class when he visited China, and he correctly concluded that the wage increases were almost certain to continue for years to come. Neutex was able to react quickly to new data impacting its offshoring decision.

Finally, the added costs of the offshoring challenges, especially those of shipping and quality problems, became very evident to top management at Neutex. As a small company, it was nimble and able to react quickly to problems as they emerged. That made the reshoring decision and the reshoring implementation easier. Clearly, Higgins provided outstanding leadership as Neutex navigated both the offshoring and reshoring. Few companies can claim they made an early "no brainer" decision to offshore, observed and counted the unforeseen costs associated with importing from a distant country, and admitted they had miscalculated and decided to reshore within 3 years of the initial decision.

GENERAL ELECTRIC

It began in 1951 as one of the finest examples of American manufacturing muscle. General Electric built an impressive industrial park to produce an array of household appliances—the company even named it "Appliance Park"—in Louisville, Kentucky. In perhaps typical GE style, it boasted a campus of six huge buildings, an independent fire department, its own power generating plant, a mile long parking lot complete with traffic lights, and eventually even a separate zip code. It would serve the growing demand for appliances as the economic recovery from WWII exploded into the US housing market. Employment in the park measured in tens of thousands, with 16,000 in 1955, and peaked at 23,000 in 1973. Then, activity at Appliance Park began to decline. By early 2011, hourly employment had plummeted to an incredible low of 1,863 workers![19]

Labor strife caused numerous interruptions in production, particularly during the 1970s and 1980s. That, coupled with the nation's industrial shift to offshoring in search of much lower wages, sealed the doom of Appliance Park for several decades.

For GE, part of the offshoring motivation was to maximize its stock price by lowering its costs. Public companies can be driven to short-term solutions like this by focusing more on previous quarterly results and less on long term growth strategies. Higher costs in Louisville, driven in part by the labor strife, led GE to move production overseas. Even with lower costs of production, diminishing business results prompted GE in 2008 to attempt to sell its appliance business. In a strangely ironic twist that benefited the remaining employees, there was no market for this business as the Great Recession began to unfold.[19] It remained in GE's possession. Nevertheless, it was sad to see such a dramatic change of direction for the historically successful company. What had made it successful in the first place?

General Electric was formed in 1892, the product of a merger of the Edison General Electric Company and the Thomson-Houston Company. This hugely successful company has manufactured everything from the simple electric fan to train locomotives and x-ray machines. 1910 saw the introduction of the first electric range; in 1930 GE began to market electric clothes washers as it expanded its offerings into the American home. The kitchen disposal, taken for granted by most of us but considered a necessity, was a 1935 GE introduction.[20]

It was not until 1942 that GE produced its first jet engine—the product that comes to mind today when many people think of GE.[20] Most people probably do not realize that as a company, GE has been assigned more than 37,000 patents![21] This is a company with innovation in its DNA. It is also a company historically entrenched in the appliance producing business.

After manufacturing a virtual laundry list of domestic products, it was shocking when the industrial giant pulled work out of Appliance Park in Kentucky and began making water heaters in China. Few people probably ever anticipated a reversal of that offshoring decision, but by 2012, the reshoring had begun in earnest in Appliance Park. Not only was the hot water heater production returning to Kentucky from China, but also other products were planned for production in the Park. High-end French door refrigerators, stainless steel dishwashers, and front-loading clothes washers and dryers were finding their production home in Louisville.[19] In addition to factors cited by other reshoring companies, including the predominant one of rising wages in China, GE had several other reshoring reasons that made it somewhat unique.

First, the adoption of Lean manufacturing and design awakened the company to the potential that existed literally in its own back yard. Beginning with the design of the water heater made in China, GE engaged a team of people to consider improvements to make the product functionally better, more convenient for the user, and easier to manufacture. Plumbers, end users, engineers, factory workers, and supervisors teamed up to improve the design as well as the production process of the water heater. Students of Lean will remember that, at its core, Lean is the reduction of waste. Assembly time of the water heaters dropped from 10 hours in China to about 2 hours in Louisville. By attacking waste in both the design of the product as well as the production processes, the team was able to wring out sufficient cost so that the selling price actually was lower after production moved to Louisville.[22] Appliance Park worker productivity in 2012 was nearly three times what it had been in the 1960s.[19]

Second, GE worked with its union, the International Union of Electrical Workers, to lower the wage base at the Louisville plant by introducing a two-tiered wage scale. New workers would enter at a substantially lower hourly wage than the remaining veterans. Initially, that lower tier represented about 70% of the factory jobs.[19] The lower overall wage cost to produce appliances in Louisville, reduced labor required for manufacturing thanks to the improvements, and increasing wages in China added up to justifying the reshoring decision.

Perhaps unexpectedly, some unions have begun embracing Lean as a job preserver instead of a job loser. On the surface, it seems incongruous that unions would support anything that reduces employee headcount. If done correctly, Lean makes sense for everyone involved. Management must demonstrate that when labor is removed as a form of waste, employees' jobs are likely to survive. Surplus personnel must be moved to other positions in the company. Otherwise, there is little to be gained by workers when they try to help eliminate waste but end up eliminating themselves! Also, unions with good strategic thinking realize that companies embracing Lean will likely restore manufacturing jobs to the United States, thereby increasing the overall number of employees. In a nutshell, fewer jobs per square foot of factory floor is better for unions than no domestic factory floors at all! While no one expects the employment at Appliance

Park to approach the 1973 level of 23,000, it did hit 3,600 by the end of 2012.[19] That was an increase of 1,700 jobs over the prior year. Things have been improving in Louisville.

Anyone familiar with labor relations in the United States is likely to be surprised by the tone of a union president during an interview in early 2012. The discussion centered on GE reshoring the hot-water heater production to the United States and the reliance on Lean initiatives to help justify the return of the work. Jerry Carney, then union president, provided his viewpoint on the traditional union focus for preserving jobs, and how it was moving in the direction for recognizing international competition and the role the union could play in really protecting jobs[23]:

> We know we have to be globally competitive. We know we can't just look at what's happening right here. We have to look at other appliance manufacturers to make sure we are competitive with them; otherwise we will lose our jobs. If I keep a closed mind and keep my eye only on my union hall, then I'm not doing my workforce any good because these jobs will leave here in a heartbeat.

If embraced by labor nationwide and if respected appropriately by management, this attitude can be a true game changer for supporting the reshoring of manufacturing. Teams working together can accomplish amazing feats, and engaging all workers to accomplish a common goal—manufacturing success—could unleash the same spirit that previously made America the undisputed manufacturing leader on the planet.

Finally, there were some serious governmental incentives—about $17 million worth. This helped to defray the nearly $1 billion outlay GE needed to ready the Louisville facility for production.[24] While some people might scream "corporate welfare" in these incentive cases, we can all agree that investing in American jobs is better than many other ways in which the money might be spent. The benefits from an increased tax base and a reduction of the societal costs of unemployment will also be positive changes.

There are other benefits of local production. Time to market from completion of an item in the plant was diminished from over 1 month to mere hours. Another benefit is the reduction in the privacy violations, or pilferage of intellectual property. Trade secrets are much easier to protect when production is all located in the United States.

In early 2011, President Obama named General Electric CEO Jeffrey Immelt to be a top outside economic advisor. Perhaps intended as a way to improve his relationship with industry, the president's choice created a firestorm of protests, along with accolades from some business groups. Many protesters took issue with the selection of someone who headed a company with a long history of offshoring jobs, a sore spot as US unemployment lingered around 10%. Data revealed that under Immelt, GE had eliminated 34,000 jobs in the United States and added 25,000 jobs overseas.[25] To many people, he seemed a poor choice to represent American industry to the Oval Office.

By bringing jobs back to the United States in 2012, Immelt was at least moving GE in an encouraging direction. His motives may have been purely financial, looking only at costs on a spreadsheet. His conclusion and the ensuing production gains at Appliance Park indicate that the reshoring trend makes sense for even one of the largest multinational companies in the world.

WINDSTREAM TECHNOLOGIES

We conclude our review of reshoring companies with a look at an emerging technology company. In the energy arena and, in particular, wind power generation, the United States does not always fare well. Shale oil production favors us because many of the most promising oil fields are within our borders, but in the production of wind turbines, we lag behind other nations. We may have the wind, but turning it into useable electrical energy more often falls to imported equipment. In that regard, WindStream Technologies is an anomaly.

Wind turbines are popular in clean energy-circles. Like hydroelectric and solar power generation, wind turbine-generated power is clean power, the result of renewable energy with little downside. There is no air pollution or water pollution, although one of the biggest concerns with wind turbines is the collateral damage to birds or bats who can become casualties of the massive and quickly turning blades.

Around the world, sprawling wind farms consisting of perhaps several hundred large turbines covering many square miles generate huge quantities of electrical power. The almost 900 turbines in northwest Indiana stand 300 feet tall, with blades 120 feet long and weighing 7 tons each.[26] The manufacture of these giants is a market dominated by non-US companies. In 2011, only one US manufacturer cracked the top 10 in the world, and that company, GE Energy, had less than 8% market share.[27]

WindStream Technologies is a small company and does not attempt to be one of the top wind turbine producers. Like many small companies, it is working a niche. Rather than focusing on the massive turbines most of us have seen, WindStream makes smaller and much less expensive turbines. Its self-proclaimed goal is to make the capture of wind energy both affordable and accessible. Communities, businesses, and even private homes are potential customers.

WindStream Technologies was founded by Dan Bates in California in 2008. He was a classic American entrepreneur, working in several different industries and starting companies along the way. Growing up near movie studios led him to his early ventures in video and sound production. He was not completely satisfied with those and migrated into sustainability technology. His interest focused on capturing wind energy and converting it into useful electricity, but on a much smaller scale than the massive wind turbines that were already doing that.[28] From an overall economic viewpoint, his timing could not have been worse. Just as his idea was blossoming into reality, the US economy was tanking into the Great Recession.

WindStream's signature product was the TurboMill, a uniquely designed wind generator made of recycled materials intended to supplement or to replace electricity from the grid. Sales opportunities existed worldwide, providing hope for significant exports. A business born in California soon moved to Indiana as a result of state and local incentives. A technology center in New Albany, Indiana, enticed the young company with an incubator opportunity. Connected to Purdue University, the incubator offered assistance in financing, marketing, business development, technology, and even space in which to work. Specifically, WindStream would begin with 3,500 square feet of incubator real estate. Bates planned to use that space for continued research and development and some initial assembly operations.[28]

Business incubators come in numerous shapes and sizes—some focused on specific types of businesses and others more general. In every case, the theme is to assist an entrepreneur to develop an idea and launch a fledgling company into an emerging successful one. By minimizing the up-front capital required for a start-up and assisting with advice in the "business" end, the incubator supplies access to the components frequently needed by new companies. The Purdue Technology Center in Albany, Indiana, offered this lure to WindStream in 2009. The Indiana Economic Development Corporation threw in more than $84,000 in training grants and the potential of another $1.5 million in tax credits.[29] The combined package was enough to convince Bates that moving to Indiana was in WindStream's best long-term interest.

When ready to begin production in December 2010, Bates looked to a Chinese factory for actual production. Why not? That was the thing to do in manufacturing at the time. Although the increasing Chinese wages wave had just begun to form, Bates had no previous experience in this area. He had no idea the game was about to change. The first WindStream order was for 35 prototype turbines, and China was selected for both speed and low cost. It may be surprising that China would have a speed advantage in development, but overseas plants are sometimes able to produce prototypes quickly. In this case, the results were catastrophic. The prototypes were totally flawed. The quality was abysmal, and some turbine parts were installed incorrectly while others simply fell off.[30] Getting quick results at low cost did not matter when these problems surfaced.

WindStream quickly moved production to other shops, and these were in the United States. China remained the supplier of some parts due to raw material availability, but to the extent possible, production moved onshore. WindStream scrutinized all the costs involved and determined that it could produce its turbines less expensively at home in the United States.

By June 2011, WindStream had secured 45,000 square feet of manufacturing space in North Vernon, Indiana, and was hiring the first 30 production workers. Starting salaries fell into the $50,000 to $100,000 a year range with benefits and even a bonus plan. Production wages ranged from $11 to $16 an hour with benefits. From the government assistance standpoint, new, well paying jobs were the goal and were the yardstick that proved WindStream was a good "investment." From a logistics standpoint, the only downside was that manufacturing would happen in North Vernon, Indiana, about 50 miles north of the New Albany corporate headquarters and site of research and development. Local North Vernon incentives drove that move.[31]

CONCLUSION

The reshoring decision has been based on many factors, and every company is unique. There is no real pattern to uncover, but some reasons keep bubbling to the surface. In the spirit of learning from others' experiences, we look next at some of the key factors in the current reshoring decisions of companies.

REFERENCES

1. Paul Gordon. Caterpillar finds Victoria, Texas, "ideal." *Journal Star,* August 12, 2010.
2. Wikipedia. Caterpillar Inc. http://en.wikipedia.org/wiki/Caterpillar_Inc
3. Caterpillar website. <http://www.caterpillar.com/company/history>
4. Richard Mertens. With end of long strike at Caterpillar, a blow to US labor movement. *Christian Science Monitor,* August 20, 2012.
5. Chris Lusvardi. Caterpillar announces Illinois projects. Pantagraph.com. http://www.pantagraph.com/news/state-and-regional/illinois/caterpillar-announces-illinois-projects/article_b05729dc-0cee-11e1-9d53-001cc4c03286.html (November 11, 2011).
6. Jeff Engel. Caterpillar 3Q profit down 44%, mining again to blame. *Business Journal Serving Greater Milwaukee,* October 23, 2013.
7. Chris Lusvardi. CAT announces more layoffs. *Business Journal of Midcentral Illinois,* May 28, 2013.
8. Caterpillar plans to cut 1,400 jobs in Belgium. *Reuters,* February 28, 2013.
9. Wikipedia. Master Lock. <http://en.wikipedia.org/wiki/Master_Lock>
10. Master Lock website. <http://www.masterlock.com/about_us/history.jsp?a=b&a=b#timeline_year_1920>
11. John Schmid. Master Lock reassessing China. JSOnline (*Milwaukee Wisconsin Journal Sentinel,* January 1, 2011).
12. William J. Holstein. Reshoring jobs. *Compass,* August, 2013. <http://compassmag.3ds.com/Cover-Story/RESHORING-JOBS>
13. John Schmid. Master Lock hailed by Obama for "insourcing." *Milwaukee Journal Sentinel,* January 11, 2012.
14. Neutex website. <http://neutexlighting.com/2013-04-15-05-54-42/optimize-with-led>
15. L. M. Sixel. From here to China and back. *Houston Chronicle,* March 7, 2012.
16. Boston Consulting Group, Inc. 2012. The US manufacturing Renaissance: How shifting global economics are creating an American comeback.
17. Connie Lewis. Neutex Lighting returns to Houston. *Houston Business Journal,* March 2, 2012.
18. AFL-CIO website. Making the lights fantastic. <http://www.aflcio.org/Features/Collaboration-at-Work/Making-the-Lights-Fantastic>
19. Charles Fishman. The insourcing boom. *The Atlantic,* January 31, 2013.
20. General Electric website. History. <http://www.ge.com/about-us/history/1935-1945>
21. The 15 most innovative companies of all time. Business Insider. <http://www.businessinsider.com/most-innovative-companies-of-all-time-2011-6#3-general-electric-13>
22. Steve Denning. Why Apple and GE are bringing back manufacturing. *Forbes,* December 7, 2012.
23. Kevin Meyer. The reshoring story of GE appliances. *Evolving Excellence,* March 3, 2012.

24. Tony Daltorio. GE's billion dollar gamble on reshoring. *Motley Fool,* April 5, 2012.
25. Shahien Nasiripour. Obama picks Jeffrey Immelt, GE CEO, to run new jobs-focused panel as GE sends jobs overseas, pays little in taxes. *Huffington Post,* January 21, 2011.
26. Jessica Nunemaker. Indiana wind farms: Wind turbines. Paperblog.com. <http://en.paperblog.com/indiana-wind-farms-wind-turbines-25300/>
27. Wikipedia. List of wind turbine manufacturers. <http://en.wikipedia.org/wiki/List_of_wind_turbine_manufacturers>
28. Lucy Pritchett. West Coast inventor Dan Bates is making his home here to work with new Purdue research park. *Business First,* May 27, 2010.
29. IN: WindStream Technologies to site new facility; create 260+ new jobs. Trade & Industry Development. <http://www.tradeandindustrydev.com/industry/alternative-energy-fuels/news/in-windstream-technologies-site-new-facility-create-260-new-j>
30. Patricia Kavilanz. Dumping China for American job shops. *CNN Money,* February 17, 2012.
31. Sharon Hamilton. Now hiring—WindStream taking applications for NV operations. PlainDealer-Sun.com, September 26, 2011.

6

Motivation to Reshore

Offshoring for manufacturers has focused primarily on costs. While the extremely low cost of labor in Third World countries has historically been the single biggest driver of this, there are other costs as well. These include the costs of compliance with environmental and regulatory matters, taxes, exchange rates, union expenses, and more. As time has unfolded, the cost differences have shrunk in many cases. Also, many offshoring companies have learned that there were other costs that they failed to notice and include in their decision to offshore. Experience is often a great teacher, particularly of unintended consequences. This chapter examines some of the significant and emerging reasons why companies are more serious than ever about reshoring.

QUALITY

For most companies in manufacturing, high quality is a price of entry into the market. Good quality is assumed. Without this, market survival is unlikely. In manufacturing, quality comes from both the materials and the processes used in making the product. In many cases, one manufacturer's process may lead to the next one's material problems. For example, a foundry that improperly processes steel castings can create a material problem for the customer that uses those castings in its products.

Engineering holds a critical role in specifying materials, and adherence is vital if the product is to have market success. Manufacturers know this and work hard to develop material specifications for their purchasing departments. Qualifying acceptable vendors and assuring that each purchased part complies may be under the control of a Quality Department.

Over time, a vendor whose products pass without issue can lull the purchasing company into complacency. Or perhaps the vendor, once qualified, is presumed to supply good parts until a problem surfaces downstream, such as when the product arrives in the hands of an end user. More than one company has learned that dealing with offshore quality problems can be significantly more difficult than dealing with a nearby supplier. It is easier to achieve and maintain high quality when the manufacturing happens locally.

One of the biggest implications for offshored quality problems is that of stock level. Since most offshoring results in significantly larger amounts of parts stocked, a problem with quality could be huge in scope. A container load of bad parts is a much bigger problem than a crate of bad parts. Once discovered, corrective action can be equally disparate based on the source. The offshored container load of bad parts represents either a massive cost of rework or a time-consuming return to the source. It may even be scrapped, depending on its value to the source. One must navigate time zone differences and cultural and language barriers, which makes corrective action difficult. Vast quantities of problem parts create much bigger headaches and being separated by long distances makes fixing the problems more difficult.

The local or nearby source with product quality problems poses a much smaller problem. As a local source, the volume of parts impacted is almost certainly smaller. Proximity aids in resolving quality problems through more convenient communication about the error, proposals for resolution, and plans for reworking or replacing parts. Generally, local sources do not present the language, cultural, or time zone barriers in discussions and planning. In some cases, a representative from the source may be able to make an on-site visit and examine the suspect product right away. Clearly, reshoring makes it easier to fix quality problems when they occur, and problems are likely smaller in scope.

Tied closely to quality problems in parts is the availability of good parts for the manufacturer; after all, the part was needed for production. Once a lot or batch of defective parts is identified, the race is on to replace them with good parts. In the case of offshored material, the stakes are higher: not only are there more defective parts, but also getting good replacement parts is probably going to take much longer. When lead times are measured in weeks or months, an outage of critical parts constitutes an emergency. Corporate reputation for timely deliveries is at stake. If any of the bad parts slipped through the system and arrived in the hands of end users, the reputation for quality parts is also at risk.

"So, what are you going to do about it?" Normally, the first question asked of a supplier when bad parts are discovered is when good parts can be available. An offshore supplier probably will not have a viable answer, but a local supplier has at least a fighting chance. Manufacturing smaller batches more quickly with a short supply chain argues for quicker delivery in an emergency. When there is a quality problem, getting good parts to resume production will occur much faster locally and will involve a smaller number of parts.

When the source is under less scrutiny and has the opportunity to practice substandard procedures, offshoring is likely to yield higher occurrences of defective parts. Many manufacturers have learned this the hard way. Overseas producers can ignore specifications and/or substitute unapproved materials, leading to rework or scrapped parts. Scarily, sometimes the matter is not discovered until end users experience problems. This constitutes an emergency and warrants an "all hands on deck" action plan to corral bad parts in the field. Simultaneously, manufacturers must coordinate with the supplier for good parts, and then wait for delivery to rush replacements through production. When locally sourced, a qualified vendor is less likely to cause such problems. In a nutshell, it is much easier to assure continuing quality from a local supplier than an offshored one.

While it may be difficult to achieve satisfaction in the United States with an uncooperative vendor in view of collecting on bad product, it can be virtually impossible with overseas vendors where there are more variables to navigate. Separated by oceans and challenged by unfamiliar language and cultures, the manufacturer must endure the burdens of operating across time zones and pilot its way through foreign legal systems. For a smaller company with little clout and limited available resources, swallowing the loss may be the path of least resistance. Just one experience like this has the capacity to sour any company's taste for offshoring. Resolving quality problems is much simpler when we are closer geographically and share the same culture and, if necessary, legal system.

PATRIOTISM

Patriotism motivates some reshoring, even when not necessarily supported by financial justification. Companies are more likely today to market products "made in America," and they sell them at higher prices than their imported cousins. We are seeing news shows and some marquee names urging American consumers to buy American and educating audiences on the positive impact on our economy and our society if we each buy a little more "made in America." For manufacturers, this marketing option can serve as a motivator to reshore.

Mobilizing American consumers to take action, even to read the origin labels on the products they buy, is a very tall order. Success is more likely if companies direct their purchasing toward American products. One corporate purchasing policy or directive to buy American can have more impact than a publicity campaign attempting to convince consumers to look first at the labels on products they are purchasing, and then to select something "made in America." Thus, start from inside the company rather than relying on consumers inspecting labels.

QUICK DELIVERY

We live in the age of instant gratification. Consider the impatience of many customers waiting in the fast food drive-through lane! Time has become perhaps our most precious commodity in Western civilization. This rings true in the world of manufacturing, also. Customers want their orders shipped quickly, and many purchase orders are awarded based more on delivery than price. A company that ships more quickly than its competition and does so dependably commands higher margins and more loyalty from its customer base. Shipping quickly becomes a competitive advantage.

In this vein of quick shipping, the supply chain is a critical piece. Offshoring depends on a long supply chain, in both time and distance. Keeping the supply chain full means extra stock at several different levels. The offshoring company must maintain a larger than average supply of offshored parts in house and must place new purchase orders early, assuming that the in-house supply may succumb to unexpectedly heavy demand and the incoming parts may take longer than expected to arrive. This stocking practice causes havoc when a quality problem arises, for the same reasons mentioned earlier. Even when the quality is acceptable, demand surges can cause outages, delaying shipments to customers. The opposite can also occur when demand plummets and the company is stuck with a huge oversupply. Large-quantity orders, a fact of life for most offshoring, result in massive swings of inventory. No one has unlimited space, so the oversupply condition can lead to warehouse rental charges and extra handling to accommodate overages.

Shorter lead times come with shorter supply chains. Companies purchasing product locally benefit from quicker delivery, smaller lot sizes, and the increased likelihood of getting rush jobs occasionally to satisfy demand surges. When demand falls off, it is easier to shut off the supply temporarily so that demand can catch up. Sourcing locally yields benefits like lowering stocked inventory and heightening the ability to meet demand surges. Reshoring allows manufacturers to respond more quickly to changing market conditions, with considerably less overstocking risk.

SHIPPING COSTS

Shipping costs are predicated on a number of factors including size and weight, but also distance. In general, the farther something must be moved, the more it costs to move it. Transoceanic costs are par for the course with offshoring, and are added to overland prices when the receiving entity is not near a seaport. In the days of cheap energy, these expenses were considered practically incidental. Oil prices have skyrocketed in recent years, and now shipping costs matter. This has led to companies not only reshoring, but also looking to regional or even local suppliers. Not only is the lead time shortened, but the shipping costs are lowered as well. Reshoring wins over offshoring on the transportation cost front.

RISING LABOR COSTS OVERSEAS

For good reason, offshoring is largely synonymous with China. In recent years, China has emerged as a huge exporter of manufactured goods, with much of that coming to the United States. Based on historically low labor costs and an abundance of human capital, China was able to emerge as a manufacturing juggernaut. Its success also led to changes, the most impactful being the Chinese labor rate, which has mushroomed in the past several years. It is expected to continue to climb by 15% to 20% each year, which will practically negate the cost advantage when factored with the American productivity advantage. It is possible that, by 2015, the effective wage rate of China will be close to that of the United States. One of the biggest motivators for offshoring, at least to China, will evaporate. The labor rate trend clearly favors reshoring.

Coupled with rising Chinese wages is the relentless advance of American factory productivity gains. Due in part to increased automation, such as robotics, and due in part to the improvements seen by companies on Lean journeys, US productivity gains make its higher priced labor more competitive with workers around the world who may have lower wages. Those lower wage workers produce far less per unit of time. In the language of Lean, it is all about removing waste from the process. As waste is taken out, the value-added portion remains and productivity climbs. Some workers may view this as taking advantage of them, but the reality is that it makes US workers more valuable than their offshored competitors and enhances their employment opportunities. So, when we consider the rapidly rising labor rates in China and the improving productivity in the United States, especially through Lean implementation, we have two more powerful reasons to reshore.

CASH

Cash tied up in inventory is of no additional value to a company. It is common for offshoring vendors to demand payment in advance. Since order quantity is typically large, this is double trouble for a company short on cash. It must invest additional cash earlier in the procurement process to purchase offshored parts or materials. Once product arrives, it takes longer to recover the cash simply because it takes longer to sell the larger quantity of product. In short, securing product offshore requires larger amounts of cash and ties it up longer. While the value of this cash may vary from company to company, clearly it is to any company's advantage to have more use of its cash more of the time. This is another strong argument for reshoring.

INTELLECTUAL PROPERTY

Intellectual property is a valuable corporate asset that offshoring puts at serious risk, depending on the offshored country. Ethics and values vary significantly from one culture to another and thus from one country to another. Presuming that other cultures share our definition of business integrity can be a serious miscalculation. History has proven that some companies in other countries use a much looser definition of integrity and act according to their definition. Learning a corporate secret and then using it to compete in the marketplace is an action that we in the United States would consider taking to court. Formally, this might look like a patent violation. When a company sets up an offshoring manufacturing operation, it may need to divulge either process or product content secrets. It does so trusting that the receiving company will maintain required confidentiality.

In some countries, using confidential information for personal or competitive advantage is not considered wrong. It may even be viewed as expected! Certainly the legal protection we enjoy in the United States does not exist in such countries. Those whose success largely depends on maintaining a technological advantage over others in their market have a lot to lose when sharing the intellectual property required to produce offshore. If offshoring companies compromise proprietary information, the impact on the original company can range from loss of market share to devastation as copies appear in the marketplace. Preserving intellectual property can bring incalculable cost savings to a manufacturer, which adds to the growing list of reasons to reshore.

CONTINUOUS IMPROVEMENT

A lack of emphasis on quick changeovers is tied to the generally larger volumes involved in offshoring. Any manufacturer formerly committed to batch production understands that the large batches spread changeover costs over a much larger base and thus are not viewed as an improvement target. Also, having plenty of stock discourages frequent changeovers. This lack of urgency to reduce setup time extends to offshoring companies, too.

When a company reshores and adopts Lean principles to be more competitive, it needs to produce lot sizes approaching one piece flow, not large batch quantities. That goal heightens the need for quick changeovers. Being sufficiently disciplined to make much smaller quantities of parts on a more frequent basis mandates less expensive setups. Time saved in setups translates into extra parts produced and also removes that psychological barrier to smaller lot sizes. When a company succeeds in reducing the setup change times, it is more likely to shrink its lot sizes continually, requiring less raw part inventory and less space required for storage. This translates into having product when it is needed by the customer without committing to massive stock quantities and the space required to maintain said stock. By removing setup waste from the system, the manufacturer lowers its cost and is more competitive.

Additionally, process improvements will remove even more waste in production, adding to the competitive advantage. When achieved domestically, such cost savings can be used to delay or avoid price increases when raw materials or overhead costs are escalating. When the process is offshored, process improvements are unlikely. Material and overhead costs are more likely to be passed on to the customer, in this case, the manufacturer. That is precisely what many offshoring companies are currently experiencing: rapidly escalating costs due to labor, material, and transportation cost increases. There is little or no potential for process improvements to offset the increases. Companies that reshore and employ Lean practices should enjoy the fruits of improved product and processes on a regular basis.

TRAVEL

The manufacturer that chooses to offshore to China will learn the lessons of its predecessors. Besides the obvious differences in language and culture, expensive and regular travel to the Chinese sites is part of the drill. Travel is expensive in both direct costs, including air fare and lodging, as well as in time and energy required to work effectively in an unfamiliar culture. A few examples specific to respecting the culture include proper participation in the nuances of introductions and dining etiquette. The Chinese business culture expects a proper recognition of sequence during introductions, wherein seniority and rank are of paramount importance. Even the exchanging of business cards retains a certain formality: The recipient of the card accepts it from the giver with both hands, indicating respect for the value of the card. Dining etiquette requires knowledge of courses and plate changes during the meal, appropriate drinking and toasting, and, as the host, paying the bill. The transportation costs, time away from the office, and costs of staying in China must all be included in the cost of offshoring. Do not neglect the costs of preparing for the travel and learning the culture! Reshoring eliminates the need for most travel costs to visit suppliers and completely removes the cultural learning requirements.

EXCHANGE RATES

Currency exchange rates have been a bone of contention among international trade debates for many years. These rates, along with regulatory burdens or lack thereof, form the basis of the "level playing field" discussions. Some countries have been rather obvious about controlling their currency exchange rate value, which leverages their own manufacturing base. In the case of China, since joining the World Trade Organization in 2001 it has been under pressure to allow its currency value to "float," or reflect market demands. As the Chinese government gradually loosened its grip, the net effect on US manufacturers has been positive. It has been correspondingly negative for the importers. Reshoring from China has never looked better.

Exchange rates fluctuate over time, and this creates uncertainty. At times the advantage can be to the imports and at other times to the exports. For the smaller company, reshoring or keeping production domestic can be more stable. When combined with the political unrest that plagues many countries with whom we trade, we become even more apprehensive. Fluctuating prices in the retail world are frustrating—just check the price at the gasoline pump! For the manufacturer, to alter price is more difficult, because long-term contracts may preclude changing the prices.

Amending price lists can be a lengthy process. For many companies, rapidly increasing material prices must be absorbed, at least initially. Since China's pricing is rapidly moving, mostly in an upward direction, reshoring offers pricing stability and, very soon, perhaps a cost advantage. Predictability is a treasure, and avoiding the shifting landscape of exchange rates is a clear benefit to reshoring.

INNOVATION

Product and process improvements generally happen best when an entire company is involved. When manufacturing is separated (i.e., offshored) from management, the functions of R&D (research and development), purchasing, engineering, product innovation, and improvement are hampered by the distance and disconnection. Many improvement ideas for both product and process come from the factory floor, but those do not happen when the manufacturing is offshored. Offshoring companies depend on the engineering and R&D departments to identify and design product improvements. They have very little input into process improvements, which could impact product improvements in some cases. Reshoring will position a company to maximize its potential to innovate and, consequently, its ability to compete based on product improvements.

CONCLUSION

There are other costs of offshoring. Some, such as the impact on getting new products to market, may be difficult to quantify. Raw material availability may be an advantage in the United States and a hindrance in an offshored situation. A shorter supply chain and avoidance of the customs bureaucracy mean less risk of loss of product or unanticipated delay. The list of reasons to reshore continues to grow.

It is very likely that a company currently offshoring some or all of its manufacturing may decide to take another look at its decision. Perhaps increasing costs drive the review, or maybe the revelation that there have been hidden costs involved that simply were unnoticed until now. In any event, once a decision is made to review, recognize that it is not a simple process. Missing steps may lead to a poor decision. The next chapter provides structure to make a good decision.

Section V

A Decision-Making Model
to Reshore...or Not

7

A 360° Approach to Making a Reshoring Decision

Making a reshoring decision begins with knowing the current condition of your offshoring situation, such as product cost, issues of working with your offshored vendor, and alignment with your mission–vision–strategy.

Let us start with product cost.

You might have gone with your current offshored source because the product or component's "advertised cost" was alluring, and you thought the offshored cost was better than what you were paying or absorbing by making the product on-shore. However, the advertised cost is seldom the only cost incurred with any purchase—for example, the Yugo.

Those of us old enough will remember the Yugo automobile that was imported from Eastern Europe in the 1980s. Its "advertised cost" was thousands of dollars less than anything offered by US manufactured cars—or any other car, for that matter. But, failures and repairs made the cost of owning the Yugo much higher than that for most other cars of its class. The point is that the advertised cost is only the beginning of your relationship with the product. As the Yugo owner, you would be intimately involved with its problems and expenses. After all, you are in the driver's seat. You have a 360° view of what it really costs to own a Yugo!

But, when buying products for resale, there are many people in the driver's seat, each with a unique view of the product and its problems and expenses. The challenge is to have each driver's inputs to develop a complete, 360°, picture of the offshored product. Think of this as opening the blind spots of your company to what the offshored product is really costing. Let us call the offshored manufacturing source the Ace Manufacturing Co., or ACE, for short.

WHO TO INVOLVE IN OPENING BLIND SPOTS

Who to involve in opening your blind spots is perhaps the most important question to answer. It is everyone in your company who is affected by the product being made by ACE. Here are a few examples:

Marketing

Marketing personnel go through great pains to identify products customers will find desirable over the competition's. They do research to understand the needs and wants of customers. Marketing also discovers trends in customers' buying decisions, such as size, functionality, color, feel, weight, price, service, and warranty. For example, if Marketing determined that customers desired a brushed metallic surface over a glossy chrome finish on a kitchen appliance, then the department would want to monitor how consistently ACE was producing the desired finish. Variants from the brushed metallic surface could have effects of lost sales, recalls, extra costs incurred in rework, and even scrap. Marketing will have inputs such as this in assessing the overall cost of working with ACE.

Engineering

While Marketing determines what customers want to buy, Engineering determines the specifications to which the product is to be made. For example:

1. Mechanical and structural elements
2. Control systems
3. Motor types
4. Output capacities
5. Input elements
6. Electrical requirements
7. Hydraulic requirements
8. Joining and assembly techniques of bolting, riveting, welding
9. Purchased parts specifications

And the list goes on.

Engineering's efforts are in vain if ACE does not conform to the requirements set forward. Engineering will want to have input regarding its assessment of ACE's ability to track and record meeting specifications.

Operations

Even though the products in question have been offshored to ACE, Operations might be involved adding services such as receiving the products, sorting them, performing incoming inspection, handling them, and performing additional processing, repackaging, shipping, and other activities. The shop personnel have perhaps the most hands-on experiences with the products. They have invaluable information regarding the condition in which products arrive and if they require unexpected attention such as handling, rework, or even worse, surprises! Our research has led to stories of products arriving with unusual odors, coated with indefinable substances that cause dermatological skin problems, and one product that contained hidden flea larvae that resulted in a breakout of a flea infestation in the shop. The shop personnel definitely have information waiting to be tapped.

Quality

Wherever the products are made, Quality has the responsibility to ensure they are made to the specifications defined by Engineering and as intended by Marketing. Since ACE is the source, Quality must interface with the company constantly to ensure that the quality plan, defined and written by Quality, is being implemented. That means on-site verification in the form of audits, incoming quality inspections, material review board activities, rework–repair–scrap decisions, issuance of corrective action requests, and follow-ups on actions. Quality will be able to provide firsthand information regarding ACE's track record on first-run quality, rework, repair, scrap, warranty, and its response to corrective action requests.

Regulatory

Regulatory will be involved when the products being made are for the medical market, human consumption, aviation, transportation, or other markets where governing agencies, inside and outside the United States, have authority over design and quality outcomes. Such agencies in the

United States are the Food and Drug Administration (FDA) and Federal Aviation Administration (FAA). In Europe, the agencies include European Medicines Agency and the European Aviation Safety Agency. In China, the agencies are the State Food and Drug Administration…and the list goes on. When ACE makes the products, these governing agencies have the authority to inspect them to determine if they were made to specification as defined by Engineering and previously approved by the regulatory agency. This includes components and subassemblies supplied by other sourcing companies as well as the manufacturing performed by ACE.

If the products do not meet the agency's inspection requirements, the agency could take several paths of corrective action. In the United States, the FDA and FAA have the power to quarantine all products in inventory, recall products already sold, and inspect ACE's manufacturing site as well as subassembly sites. They may then issue corrective action requests, putting your company on probation; at the worst, they can shut down your facility. Obviously, any of these actions could have onerous consequences and could put your company out of business. Regulatory is obviously very concerned about ACE's ability to meet and pass all governing agencies' rigorous examinations of its performance and the department will have valuable input on ACE's ability to meet all regulatory agencies' scrutinizing oversight.

Sales

Sales can have either an easy or a very difficult job. When Marketing does its homework right and manufacturing performs as planned, the old cliché is also right: The products fly off the shelf. However, if either fails, then Sales's job can be very difficult. Whether sales are conducted directly or via sales representatives, Sales will have valuable information about how customers feel about the products sourced to ACE. Good salespeople and distributors will keep records showing sales by product, by customer, and by date, and they will be able to provide timely information regarding the track records of products made by ACE. Tapping into their data source will provide insight to the total cost of working with ACE, especially if the sales and distribution people are putting a lot of time into selling ACE-made products and are getting little in return or, even worse, customers are buying ACE-made products but are complaining about them or returning them for refund or replacement under warranty.

Customer Service

Customer Service personnel will be able to give their feedback on the number of customers complaining about ACE-made products or calling for instructions on how to use the product. Customer Service is usually at the forefront of facing angry customers wanting to know how to use products, complaining about them, or wanting to return them. If customers want to return products, a series of actions follow that will incur a domino effect of additional costs to your company. These might include providing complimentary reshipping back to the company, sorting packages at the receiving dock, and deciding what to do with the opened packages. A variety of other actions might include sending product to be reworked, repaired, or scrapped, or sending the product back to ACE, R&D, Engineering, or Quality for evaluation or analysis. Obviously, the dominos keep falling, adding costs, until the customer is once again happy. Many of these "domino costs" are often not anticipated and the costs are not captured but certainly do add to the cost of doing business with ACE. How would you know unless you asked for Customer Service's input?

Warranty

Warranty actions on ACE-made products will certainly add to the costs of doing business with ACE. The warranty department should have accurate records by customer, action taken, and, hopefully, costs incurred. The actions will typically be repair and return, replace, or reduce price. Again, the process of making a customer happy will add to the cost of doing business with ACE. Warranty's information will add to your understanding of how ACE stacks up to being a reliable source to make your products.

Accounting

Accounting will have the purchasing numbers for ACE-made products, such as date and quantity ordered from ACE, purchase price, the date ACE was paid, and amount paid. Accounting will also have sales data, such as sales by date and by customer, quantity sold, date shipped, sales price, date revenue was received, and how much was received. These data will provide information about the flow of cash, from expenses to revenues, and the time lag between expenses and revenues. Gross profits can be determined from the data as well as the gross cash conversion cycle.

The controller function of Accounting should have cost data on ACE-made products beyond the simple purchased price, such as additional costs incurred by the various departments previously discussed. The controller will need to keep a keen eye on these costs, as many will be unaccounted for or buried in overhead. Some examples are the flea infestation in the shop, sorting through returned items from customers, travel to ACE to approve manufacturing processes and quality procedures, conference calls to ACE, dealing with regulatory agencies, repairing, reworking, return postage, etc. The controller should have data on all these additional costs itemized by ACE-made products. Obviously, Accounting has abundant information to provide concerning the costs of working with ACE.

Finance

Finance will have information regarding the cost of capital, both now and forecasted, as well as determining whether to use cash or to borrow in order to finance a change in source for ACE-made products. There will definitely be a cost incurred for such a change wherever the source change is made, particularly a decision to bring the products in house. Finance must also be involved in deciding the cost of doing business with ACE.

Purchasing

Let us not forget Purchasing; after all, it is this group that deals most frequently with sources, including ACE. The department places orders, negotiates price and terms, follows up on shipments, and a myriad of other things that Purchasing must do to get the order to the door on time. Purchasing will have developed a history of encounters with ACE and have an opinion of the other costs of working with ACE. They are the least to be left out of the process of opening your costing blind spots.

Customers

Your company may believe that ACE is the preferred source to make your products, but you need to know what your customers think of ACE-made products. Even though you have all the previously defined examples of cost-incurring activities, there is nothing better than asking those who both buy and experience your ACE-made product or make a "no purchase decision." They buy based on opinions or hearsay from others who have bought the product, from information they have gathered through social media, and by word of mouth. Harley Davidson is the king of going to and listening to the voices of its customers; you should do the same. Marketing is the department to initiate this activity and bring back what your customers like and do not like about the ACE-made product.

Making an informed and accurate reshoring decision will require a fair amount of time and effort on many of the parties mentioned previously. We know there is a loud groan coming from the readers just about now and we understand your pain, because we are manufacturing businesspeople, too. Everyone is busy and does not have the time to spend on future activities. A way to make the time and effort more palatable is to remember why you are considering reshoring your product or products. It is because the initial plan for offshoring is not working as well today as it did previously. You and your people are already spending time with many of the issues we have discussed. If you want to have the issues go away and not return, and if you want to make sure your new resourcing decision is sound, you and your people will have to take the time and make the effort. Here are a few old sayings that you will remember:

> "Insanity is doing the same thing over and over again and expecting different results" (attributed to Albert Einstein).

> "Measure twice, cut once."

> "A stitch in time saves nine."

In other words, if you do not make a change, the offshoring problems and costs will continue, and if you do make a change, you had better make the best reshoring decision you can.

We have developed a three-phase model, Figure 7.1, for making your reshoring decision that is guaranteed to provide you with all the information you will need either to bring your manufacturing back home or to leave it offshored. All phases of the model will be explained in the next chapters. We wish you good luck in making your decision!

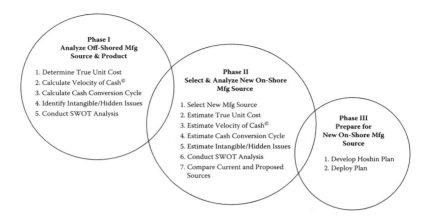

FIGURE 7.1
Reshoring Decision-Making Model©.

PHASE I: ANALYZE THE CURRENT OFFSHORED MANUFACTURING SOURCE

Phase I of the Reshoring Decision-Making Model©, as illustrated in the model, is to analyze the current offshored manufacturing source. We will demonstrate the steps by following the manufacturing, shipping, receiving, and sales of the ACE-made product to your facility.

Step 1. Determine the True Unit Cost of the Offshored Product

If you traced the trail of the ACE-made product—let us call it the ACE 41—from placing the order to selling it, you will probably find the true cost is more than simply the price listed on the invoice. Our ACE 41 has a purchase price of $7.50 per unit when bought in shipment quantities of 7,500 parts, but there are additional costs that will have to be considered to determine its true unit cost.

If you buy from an importing agency, the additional costs may be hidden within the purchase price. However, it is to your advantage to have all additional costs such as taxes, fees, and other expenses itemized so that you can monitor their changing, as they are likely to do. A few examples of additional costs include:

- Special nongovernmental fees from the sourcing country are sometimes called gratuities, graft, gifts, palm greasers, and special fees to get the ACE 41s into the shipping container and onto the ship. It is not uncommon for containers to be held hostage until the special fees are collected, thus increasing lead time in addition to increasing product costs.
  — The ACE 41 has been averaging $500.00 in special fees per shipment order of 7,500 parts.
- Shipping costs: ocean freight costs have escalated from China and continue to increase as the cost of oil increases. Knowing your cost per container/batch/order will reveal the unit shipping cost for the ACE 41s. Shipping costs are unpredictable and fluctuate at the will of the market.
  — The ACE 41 has been averaging $3,750.00 in shipping costs per shipment order of 7,500 parts.
- Value-added tax (VAT) is the tax paid to the government for the portion of manufacturing you have contributed during the ACE 41's entire manufacturing process. China began its VAT in 1984 and it continues to be a major revenue raiser for the People's Republic. The ACE 41 is subject to the VAT and it must be included to determine its true unit cost.
  — The ACE 41 has been averaging $885.00 in VAT per shipment order of 7,500 parts.
- Customs, tariffs, and import duties are taxes on specific products for a variety of reasons, but usually to generate revenue for the importing country. Tariffs on imported goods were begun by the US government in 1789 when George Washington signed the Tariff Act to collect money to pay for the debt incurred during the American Revolutionary War and to begin our country on a sound financial footing. Tariffs are also used to protect the importing country or a specific business. For example, when Harley Davidson was struggling to compete with Japanese motorcycles in the 1970s, it asked the US government to impose a stiff import duty on motorcycles greater than 750 cc's, which reduced the number of motorcycles of that size entering the country. Later, when the company began competing more effectively, it asked the government to withdraw the tariff. You will want to know the import duties and taxes for the ACE 41, too.
  — The ACE 41 has been averaging $850.00 in import duties per shipment order of 7,500 parts.

- Marine insurance: the ACE 41s, loaded in shipping containers, will be subjected to the rocking and bumping that occurs while the container ship is at sea and while your container is being on- and offloaded. Shipping damage is likely and marine insurance is another cost to cover the ACE 41s.
  — The ACE 41 has been averaging $667.00 in marine insurance per shipment order of 7,500 parts.
- Rail and trucking fees: once the containers are offloaded from the ship they must be transported to you via rail and/or trucking. The farther away you are from the shipping destination, of course, the more costly it will be to get the ACE 41s to you.
  — The ACE 41 has been averaging $1,200.00 for rail and $1,050.00 for trucking fees per shipment order of 7,500 parts.

Once the ACE 41s arrive at your facility there will be other costs; some will be tracked specifically to the ACE 41s, but are more likely not to be tracked. Again, it is to your advantage to be aware of these incremental costs for the ACE 41s in order to know its true unit cost. For example:

- Truck offloading cost occurs whether your products are made thousands of miles away or across town.
  — The ACE 41 has been averaging $500.00 in truck offloading per shipment order of 7,500 parts.
- Storage: large lot sizes are the norm for products made offshore and they must be stored somewhere. You might have rented space or a have a location at your facility to keep the ACE 41s until they are needed for further manufacturing or sale. You might even have to move the ACE 41s from storage place to place to make room for other products during their stay at your plant.
  — The ACE 41 has been averaging $750.00 in storage per shipment order of 7,500 parts.
- Inspection: since you are not in direct control of the manufacturing process, regardless of the instructions and procedures you have given to ACE, there must be a method to ensure that ACE 41s have been made to your specifications before they are in the hands of the customer. A sampling inspection plan is too risky since the probability is high that defective parts might go undetected. As a result, until the defect rate falls close to zero, a 100% inspection plan is the only safe way to go.

— The ACE 41 has been averaging 100% receiving inspection at
$0.75 per part per shipment order of 7,500 parts.

- Handling: many offshored products require extra handling from time
to time and usually without prior notification. Removing unwanted
labels, wrappings, and packaging material; sorting through different
parts, unknown films, and liquids, etc. must all be dealt with if they
arrive with the ACE 41s.
  — The ACE 41 has been averaging 25% handling cost at $2.00 per
  part per shipment order of 7,500 parts.

- Rework or scrap: if all goes right, the ACE 41s will arrive in perfect
condition, but if not, they will require being reworked or scrapped.
Rework is returning the ACE 41 to its specified condition, which
could entail many different scenarios; some could add untold costs.
The reason for investing extraordinary rework costs might be
because you will have to wait for another long delivery lead-time to
replenish the wrongly manufactured ACE 41s. Scrapping is required
when the rework cost becomes prohibitive or if rework is impossible.
  — The ACE 41 has been averaging 10% rework at $5.00 per part and
  5% scrap at $15.00 per part per shipment order of 7,500 parts.

- Unexpected expenses are the unpleasant surprises that may accompany the ACE 41s. Here are a couple true stories. A flea infestation
was traced to a shipment of concrete backer boards from China, the
"low-cost provider." The fleas wrought havoc throughout the entire
factory of this company. Work was disrupted as employees itched,
scratched, complained, and shooed away the fleas. Extermination
companies were unsuccessful in getting rid of the fleas, notwith-
standing being paid for their services. The problem persisted until
finally the fleas died off. In another company making heavy-duty
industrial components, the unexpected surprise occurred when
an engineer handled some parts received from China that had an
unknown film coating them. The engineer developed a case of dermatitis that persisted for months, causing medical expenses and
personal discomfort. Be aware of the unexpected surprises; they can
be very costly. Because these have been isolated cases, they have not
been included in extra costs for the ACE 41.

You might be surprised when compiling the true unit cost of the ACE
41 made at its current source. Of course, as you have probably discovered,
many of the costs are not tracked or cannot be practically tracked. That

TABLE 7.1

Additional Costs before Receiving Parts—ACE 41

Item	Avg. Cost per Shipment	Avg. Cost per Part
Gratuities—graft	$500.00	$0.066
Transocean shipping	$3,750.00	$0.500
Value-added tax	$885.00	$0.118
Customs/tariff	$850.00	$0.113
Marine insurance	$667.00	$0.089
Rail transportation	$1,200.00	$0.160
Truck transportation	$1,050.00	$0.140
Additional cost per part		**$1.19**

TABLE 7.2

Additional Costs after Receiving Parts—ACE 41

Item	Avg. Cost per Shipment	Frequency of Occurrence	Avg. Total Cost per Shipment	Avg. Cost per Part
Truck offloading	$500.00	Each shipment	$500.00	$0.067
Storage	$750.00	Each shipment	$750.00	$0.100
Inspection	$0.75 per part	100% of all parts	$5,625.00	$0.750
Handling	$2.00 per part	25% of all parts	$3,750.00	$0.500
Rework	$5.00 per part	10% of all parts	$3,750.00	$0.500
Scrap	$15.00 per part	5% of all parts	$5,625.00	$0.750
Additional cost per part				**$2.67**

does not mean any or all of these listed costs are not attributed to the ACE 41. It surely is not your intent to bury your head in the sand, but it is important for you to know what the ACE 41 is really costing you. Tables 7.1 and 7.2 tally the additional average costs to the ACE 41 before and after being received at your facility and calculate the additional average cost per part. Table 7.3 adds the additional costs to the purchased price of the ACE 41 to disclose its true average unit cost.

Our example could have included many other costs that increase the true cost of the ACE 41, such as flea infestations, visits to the factory offshore, conference calls to work through problems, and extra overhead to handle the offshored products. However, the point is clearly made: The purchased price is not the whole unit cost of the ACE 41.

TABLE 7.3

True Average Unit Cost—ACE 41

Purchased price per part	$7.50
Additional cost per part	
Before receiving parts	$1.19
After receiving parts	$2.67
True average unit cost	**$11.3536**

Step 2. Calculate the Offshored Product's Velocity of Cash©

Our research in writing this book has shown the need for a financial model that is different from the generally accepted accounting principles (GAAP) models and calculations, but supplements them in terms that most manufacturing employees can relate to better. The need arises for nonfinancial workers, who are the vast majority in manufacturing companies, to have a way of understanding in terms with which they are more familiar, the financial value of products sourced from companies like ACE. We have tested our new financial model, Velocity of Cash©, with much enthusiasm. Its genesis is the popularity of describing how fast things go. Here are just few examples:

- Autos: the Porsche 911 GT3 has a top speed of 195 miles per hour.
- Race cars: Paul Tracy's Indy car recorded a speed of 256 miles per hour at the Michigan International Speedway.
- NASCAR: Danica Patrick's race car can clock 196.220 miles per hour.
- Motorcycles: the Hyabusa motorcycle can reach a top speed of 161 miles per hour.
- Jets: the F16 fighter has a combat mission fight speed of Mach 1.6 (1,217.8 miles per hour).
- Bullet trains: the original bullet train in Japan hit speeds of 185 miles per hour.

Thinking about how fast things go also presents a visual image and provides discussion topics that are appealing. When compared to EBITDA (earnings before interest, taxes, depreciation, and amortization), gross margin per FTE (full-time employee), ROI (return on investment), etc., Velocity of Cash is likely to appeal more to the vast majority of the company's personnel. That is why we have chosen to include it with the other, more traditional models.

Velocity of Cash (VOC) is simply how fast the ACE 41 is making money for the company. The units of measure are similar to speed's miles per hour; Velocity of Cash is measured in dollars per day. To calculate the VOC for the ACE 41 the following information is required:

- Purchasing:
    - Date the order is placed for the ACE 41s
    - Quantity of ACE 41s ordered
    - Unit or lot price of the ACE 41s
    - Terms of payment agreed to for the ACE 41s
    - Date your company paid for the ACE 41s
- Space and time costs between ACE and your company (Note: Some or all of these may be included in your purchase price as was described in determining the true unit cost of the ACE 41.):
    - Export taxes from the sourcing country
    - Transportation costs to shipping origin
    - Customs taxes
    - Excise taxes
    - Dock fees
    - Shipping costs to US POA (port of authority)
    - Dock fees
    - Rail costs
    - Trucking costs
    - Date the ACE 41s arrive at your company
    - Quantity of the ACE 41s that arrive at your company
- Activities that are performed by your company in order to sell the ACE 41s (Note: Some or all of these may not apply or are not tracked for cost.):
    - Receiving/handling
    - Unpacking
    - Sorting
    - Repacking
    - Shipping
    - Reworking
    - Scrapping
- Sales:
    - Note: Since products are sold to a variety of customers at different times, with different quantities, with differing terms, the

following information may have to be bundled for convenience at the expense of total accuracy:
- – Date, quantity, and price of ACE 41 sales
- – Dollar amount and date received for the ACE 41s sold

For our ACE 41s made offshore, we have the scenarios as shown in Tables 7.4, 7.5, and 7.6 using information from the previous true unit cost exercise. Note, for sake of simplicity and demonstration purposes, the scenario data are considered constant throughout the duration of the offshoring.

When calculating the Velocity of Cash, it helps to have a visual representation of just how fast the ACE 41 is making money for your company. The method developed by the authors is to use a Microsoft Excel spreadsheet (Figure 7.2) that has graphing capabilities. The data are represented as shown in Figure 7.3 based on the ACE 41 offshoring scenario:

TABLE 7.4

Purchasing Data—ACE 41

Purchase price per unit	$7.50
Order quantity	7,500
Payment terms	Payment due at time of order
Lead time of parts	15 wks. after placing order

TABLE 7.5

Sales Data—ACE 41

Weekly sales	500 ACE 41s
Selling price	$15.00 per ACE 41
Terms	4 wks. payment after placing order

TABLE 7.6

True Average Unit Cost—ACE 41

Purchased price per part	$7.50
Additional cost per part	
Before receiving parts	$1.19
After receiving parts	$2.67
True average unit cost	**$11.3536**

Week	Order Parts	Inventory Rcv Net Inv / Inv Quan	Acc Pay Booked	Acc Pay Paid	Off-Shoring Before Receiving Parts	Off-Shoring After Receiving Parts	Weekly Sales	Acc Rcv Booked	Acc Rcv Rcv'd	Acc Rcv Cumulative	Daily Profit	Cumulative Profit
0	#1	7500 7500	$56,250	$56,250							-$56,250	-$56,250
1		7000									$0	-$56,250
2		6500									$0	-$56,250
3		6000									$0	-$56,250
4		5500			Graft $500						-$500	-$56,750
5		5000			Shipping $3,750						-$3,750	-$60,500
6		4500			VAT $885						-$885	-$61,385
7		4000			Marine Ins $667						-$667	-$62,052
8		3500									$0	-$62,052
9		3000									$0	-$62,052
10		2500									$0	-$62,052
11		2000			Customs $850						-$850	-$62,902
12		1500			Rail $1,200						-$1,200	-$64,102
13	#2	7500 8500			Truck $1,050		500	$7,500		7,500	-$1,050	-$65,152
14		8000	$56,250	$56,250			500	$7,500		15,000	-$56,250	-$121,402
15		7500				Unload $500	500	$7,500	7,500	22,500	-$500	-$121,902
16		7000				Inspect $5,625	500	$7,500	7,500	30,000	-$6,125	-$128,027
17		6500				Handling $3,750	500	$7,500	7,500	30,000	-$7,500	-$135,527
18		6000				Rework $5,625	500	$7,500	7,500	30,000	-$4,635	-$140,162
19		5500				Scrap $750	500	$7,500	7,500	30,000	-$6,292	-$146,454
20		5000			Graft $500		500	$7,500	7,500	30,000	$6,750	-$139,704
21		4500			Shipping $3,750		500	$7,500	7,500	30,000	$7,500	-$132,204
22		4000			VAT $885		500	$7,500	7,500	30,000	$7,500	-$124,704
23		3500			Marine Ins $667		500	$7,500	7,500	30,000	$6,650	-$118,054
24		3000			Customs $850		500	$7,500	7,500	30,000	$6,300	-$111,754
25		2500			Rail $1,200		500	$7,500	7,500	30,000	$6,450	-$105,304
26		2000			Truck $1,050		500	$7,500	7,500	30,000	$7,500	-$97,804
27		1500					500	$7,500	7,500	30,000	$7,500	-$90,304
28	#3	7500 8500	$56,250	$56,250			500	$7,500	7,500	30,000	-$49,250	-$139,554
29		8000				Unload $500	500	$7,500	7,500	30,000	$1,875	-$137,679
30		7500				Inspect $5,625	500	$7,500	7,500	30,000	$3,750	-$133,929
31		7000				Handling $3,750	500	$7,500	7,500	30,000	$3,250	-$130,679
32		6500				Rework $5,625	500	$7,500	7,500	30,000	-$1,875	-$132,554
33		6000				Scrap $750	500	$7,500	7,500	30,000	$5,865	-$126,689
34		5500			Graft $500		500	$7,500	7,500	30,000	$6,833	-$119,856
35		5000			Shipping $3,750		500	$7,500	7,500	30,000	$7,500	-$112,356
36		4500			VAT $885		500	$7,500	7,500	30,000	$7,500	-$104,856
37		4000			Marine Ins $667		500	$7,500	7,500	30,000	$7,500	-$97,356
38		3500					500	$7,500	7,500	30,000	$3,750	-$93,606
39		3000					500	$7,500	7,500	30,000	$6,650	-$86,956
40		2500			Customs $850		500	$7,500	7,500	30,000	$6,300	-$80,656
41		2000			Rail $1,200		500	$7,500	7,500	30,000	$6,450	-$74,206
42		1500			Truck $1,050		500	$7,500	7,500	30,000	$7,500	-$66,706
43	#4	7500 8500	$56,250	$56,250			500	$7,500	7,500	30,000	-$48,750	-$115,456
44		8000				Unload $500	500	$7,500	7,500	30,000	$7,000	-$108,456
45		7500				Inspect $5,625	500	$7,500	7,500	30,000	$1,875	-$106,581
46		7000				Handling $3,750	500	$7,500	7,500	30,000	$3,750	-$102,831
47		6500				Rework $5,625	500	$7,500	7,500	30,000	$3,250	-$99,581
48		6000				Scrap $750	500	$7,500	7,500	30,000	$990	-$98,591
49		5500					500	$7,500	7,500	30,000	$6,083	-$92,508
50		5000					500	$7,500	7,500	30,000	$7,500	-$85,008
51		4500					500	$7,500	7,500	30,000	$7,500	-$77,508
52		4000					500	$7,500	7,500	30,000	$7,500	-$70,008
53		3500					500	$7,500	7,500	30,000	$7,500	-$62,508
54		3000					500	$7,500	7,500	30,000	$7,500	-$55,008

FIGURE 7.2
Offshored ACE 41 activity.

The graph of how money flows for the ACE 41 is shown in Figure 7.3, its weekly cumulative profit. There are a few elements of the graph worth noting. Notice the dip in the early stages of offshoring and the "sawtooth effect," which occurs throughout the offshoring process due the combination of:

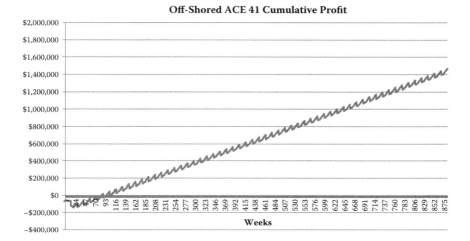

FIGURE 7.3
Offshored ACE 41 cumulative profit.

1. Extreme purchasing terms, "payment is due at time of order"
2. Extremely long 15-week lead time, from time of order, because of manufacturing lag time to complete the 7,500 part order and shipping and transportation times
3. Very large order quantity of 7,500 ACE 41s to compensate for the long lead time

The ACE 41s are not in the black until week 95. And thereafter the Velocity of Cash of ACE 41s goes through a cycle of falling off the cliff when payment is made for the enormous 7,500 piece order and then ratchets up to sell them off. This can hardly be what would be called high velocity; the ACE 41s go backward before they inch forward! This is countered, however, by the total cost of the ACE 41s, which must have been attractive initially for the company to offshore them.

The calculation for the Velocity of Cash is actually quite simple, which is its objective in the first place! The calculation is the slope of the cumulative profit line, as shown in Table 7.7.

Our ACE 41s are making $384.64 per day for our company. We will compare this to other options in Phase II.

TABLE 7.7

Velocity of Cash Calculation—ACE 41

Velocity of cash offshored ACE 41	=	(Cum. profit @ time period 2 − Cum. profit @ time period 1)		
		(Time period 2 − Time period 1)		
Cum. profit @ time period 2	=	$1,455,782	Time period 2	= Day 4,400
Cum. profit @ time period 1	=	$ 686,511	Time period 1	= Day 2,400
Subtracting 1 from 2	=	$ 769,271		2,000 Days
Velocity of cash offshored ACE 41	=	$796, 271		
		2,000 Days		
		$384.64 per Day		

Step 3. Calculate the Offshored Product's Cash Conversion Cycle

Most people are familiar with another performance element that will provide additional information and, if omitted, will not tell the whole story. For example, the bullet train has a velocity of 185 miles per hour, but how quickly it gets there is important to know, too! This author rode on the bullet train in Japan and knows from personal experience that, from a standstill, it is a gradual increase from 0 mph to its terminal speed of 185 mph. Contrast this to the commonly used performance metric of "0 to 60 mph" recorded for most sport vehicles like motorcycles and sports cars; the lower the "0 to 60" time is, the more impressive. For example, the Suzuki Hyabusa has a 2.47 second 0 to 60; the Porsche 911 GT3 does 0 to 60 in 3.3 seconds and the F16 has a 0 to 60 in about 4.4 seconds. While there is no 0 to 60 specification for the bullet train, it is a long way from the ones just mentioned, although it has an impressive top speed.

The 0 to 60 rating indicates how quickly the vehicles get to their speed of, in this case, 60 mph. The measure for how quickly the ACE 41 gets to its Velocity of Cash of $384.64 per day is found in the cash conversion cycle. First, an explanation of the cash conversion cycle will be helpful.

All products are bought under terms specified by the seller. When you go to a retail store and buy products, you typically pay at the time of purchase. You could try to talk the cashier into letting you pay a week or so later for the book or suntan oil you are buying, but that probably will not work. However, when businesses buy products or raw materials, the seller will have "terms and conditions" specified for the buyer in making payment. Common terms are "payment due 30 days after placing order,"

TABLE 7.8

Cash Conversion Cycle Examples

Receivable Terms (days)	−	Payable Terms (days)	=	Difference (days)	Comments
30	–	30	=	0	This is a *balanced* situation.
30	–	60	=	–30	This is an *advantageous* situation for your business. You are paying for your products and raw materials 30 days later than your customers are paying you.
60	–	30	=	30	This is a *disadvantageous* situation as you are paying for your products and raw materials 30 days sooner than your customers are paying you.

"payment due 30 days after receipt," "collect on delivery" (COD), and so on. As a result, in business transactions, there is an agreement between the buyer and seller regarding payment and receipt. Obviously, buyers will want longer paying terms and sellers will want shorter collecting terms.

For starters, the cash conversion cycle simply asks these questions of the business buying products and/or raw materials: "What are the receivable terms, in days, you are asking your customers to pay for your products, what are the payable terms, in days, you are paying for your products and raw materials, and what is the difference in days?" Consider Table 7.8.

However, another factor must be considered to complete the cash conversion cycle calculation: the quantity of products placed per order. The best scenario is to order just the quantity needed for production or resale. However, the order quantity will depend upon your distance from the supplier (i.e., the farther away you are from your supplier, the longer the lead time will be to get the products to you and, as a result, you will place a larger order quantity). When you receive the products they become part of your inventory and the quantity is measured in terms of the number of days on hand waiting to be sold. The term is inventory days on hand, or inventory days for short. The products in inventory increase the length of time from receiving payment for the products to having paid for them. Table 7.9 shows the total cash conversion cycle for the three previous examples.

Receivable and payment terms obviously affect the cash conversion cycle length, but the greatest factor, by far, is the amount of inventory days on hand.

TABLE 7.9

Cash Conversion Cycle Examples with Inventory Days

Receivable Terms (days)	−	Payable Terms (days)	+	Inventory (days)	=	Cash Conversion Cycle (days)
30	−	30	+	1	=	1
30	−	30	+	500	=	500
30	−	30	+	1,000	=	1,000
30	−	60	+	1	=	−29
30	−	60	+	500	=	470
30	−	60	+	1,000	=	970
60	−	30	+	1	=	31
60	−	30	+	500	=	530
60	−	30	+	1,000	=	1,030

These examples are snapshots in time to make the explanation easy to understand. However, in the real world, everything is not so cut and dried. Customers do not always pay on time, orders are placed randomly, and to calculate the cash conversion cycle properly, averages are used, usually quarterly.

Returning to the ACE 41 terms, payment due at time of order or payable terms of 0 days, the Ace Manufacturing Co. wants its money up front. This is not uncommon for offshoring manufacturing companies, especially those in China. The order quantity for the ACE 41s is dependent upon:

1. The lead time, from time of placing the order to the time of receiving the order (15 weeks)
2. The order size and quantity capacity of the shipping container (7,500 ACE 41s)
3. The sales volume (500 ACE 41s per week)

All three combine to arrive at the proper order quantity, in this case 7,500. See Table 7.10.

TABLE 7.10

Purchasing Terms—ACE 41

Purchase price per unit	$7.50
Order quantity	7,500
Payment terms	Payment due at time of order
Lead time of parts	15 wks. after placing order

TABLE 7.11

Selling Terms—ACE 41

Sales	500 ACE 41s per wk.
Selling price	$15 each
Receivable terms	Due 4 wks. after placing order

In our example, the ACE 41s sell at the rate of 500 units per week for a selling price of $15 each. The receivable terms are 4 weeks or essentially 30 days after placing the order, as shown in Table 7.11

To determine the cash conversion cycle for the ACE 41, we must determine the average receivable days, the average payable days, and the average inventory days. Because of the start-up dip in cumulative revenue during the early weeks of the offshoring, as shown in Figure 7.4, we will use a 13-week quarter average after the cumulative revenue has moved into the positive range: weeks 118 through 130, as shown in Figure 7.5.

The average receivable, payable, and inventory day calculations are shown in Table 7.12. Note: Total cost per unit is the true unit cost of the ACE 41 as described earlier with the exception of not including the one-time occurrences of the flea infestation, dermatitis, and bad smell cases.

Inserting the average receivable days, average payable days, and average inventory days to the calculation in Table 7.13 shows the offshored ACE 41's cash conversion cycle of 75 days; its 0 to 60 time is quite slow!

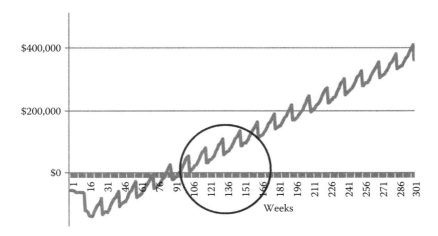

FIGURE 7.4
Start-up dip in cumulative revenue—ACE 41.

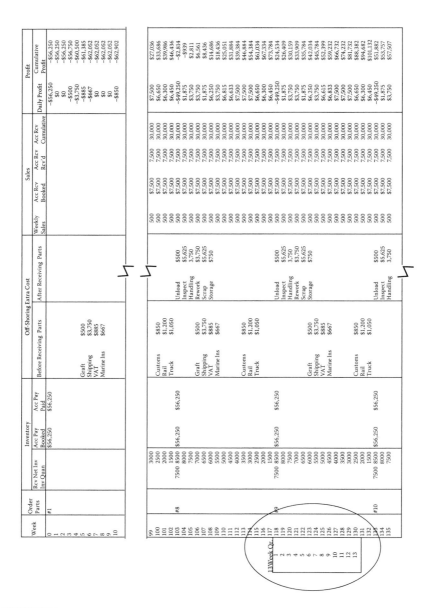

FIGURE 7.5
Thirteen-week quarter to determine quarterly averages—ACE 41.

TABLE 7.12

Cash Conversion Cycle Calculation—ACE 41

Avg. Receivable Days	=	Avg. Receivables for the Quarter ($)	÷	Sales per Day ($)
	=	$30,000	÷	$7,500 per wk. ÷ 5 days per wk. = $1,500 per day
Avg. receivable days	=	**20.00 Days**		
Avg. payable days	=	Avg. payables for the quarter ($)	÷	Purchases per day ($ per day)
	=	$00 since the terms are pay upon order	÷	7,500 units per order × $7.50 per unit ÷ 15 wks. per order ÷ 5 days per wk. = $750 per day
Avg. Payable Days	=	**0 Days**		
Avg. inventory days	=	Avg. inventory for quarter ($)	÷	Cost of goods sold per day ($ per day)
	=	5,500 avg. units per wk. × $11.3536 total cost per unit = $62,444.80	÷	500 units per wk. × $11.3536 total cost per unit ÷ 5 days per wk. = $1,135.36 per day
Avg. inventory days	=	**55.00 Days**		

TABLE 7.13

Cash Conversion Cycle Results—ACE 41

Avg. Receivable Days	−	Avg. Payable Days	+	Avg. Inventory Days	=	Cash Conversion Cycle Days
20.00	−	0	+	55.00	=	75.00

We will later see how this compares to the option of reshoring the ACE 41, making it in the United States, in phase II of the Reshoring Decision-Making Model.

Step 4. Identify the Intangible and Hidden Issues That the Offshored Product Is Causing

We have collected two very valuable elements of the offshored ACE 41, its Velocity of Cash of $385 per day and its cash conversion cycle of 75 days. These tell us the rate at which cash is being generated by the ACE 41 and its 0 to 60 rate, so to speak. We encourage more financial models to be explored for your own ACE 41, if they can be isolated for the ACE 41. In our opinion, the more data the better, which takes us to step 4 of Phase I: identifying the intangible and hidden issues that the ACE 41 is causing.

There are two types of data to describe and to contrast almost anything: quantitative data and qualitative data. Quantitative data are stated in terms of numbers that can be collected, calculated, analyzed, and so forth. The Velocity of Cash and the cash conversion cycle are quantitative data. They are irrefutable, although the manner in which they are collected and interpreted is not. For example, when we discussed speed of motor vehicles, the manner in which the speed was detected could be questioned (e.g., whether a radar gun was used to detect the speed, whether the radar gun had been calibrated recently, whether the calibrating method was verified, how the radar gun was used, etc.). However, if the same radar gun was used in the same manner to measure two of our cars (e.g., Paul Tracy's Indy car (256 mph) and the Porsche (195 mph)) those data can be said to be irrefutable that the Indy car is faster by 61 mph. Quantitative data are generally valued more than qualitative data.

Qualitative data are opinions that describe things more than measure them. It can be difficult to assign numbers to them. For example, we could describe the Porsche as beautiful, sleek, modern, road hugging, etc., but without numbers to back them up they become qualitative versus quantitative. But, just because qualitative data are not numeric does not mean they are not important. In fact, think about how most of our personal decisions are made. We choose our mates based almost solely on qualitative data. Cars are bought on quantitative data in part, but it is the qualitative data of beauty, ambiance, and that "certain feeling" that often influence us to make a buying decision.

So, just as the combination of quantitative and qualitative data is important in making the decision to buy the right car or to choose a mate, they are important to make the decision to reshore...or not to reshore. This is where step 4 comes in—collecting qualitative data to augment and supplement the quantitative data we have with the Velocity of Cash and cash conversion cycle for the offshored ACE 41.

The qualitative data we want to collect have to do with the intangible and hidden issues the ACE 41 is causing. From our research, we found that companies have huge blind spots concerning not only the true profitability of offshoring, but also the intangible and hidden issues their offshored products might be causing. As we discussed earlier, erring on the side of involving too many people is better than erring on the other side of involving too few. Again, the idea of more is better will provide a more holistic picture and thus more data upon which to make decisions.

We tested several methods of collecting qualitative data ranging from interviewing individuals and departments, sending out requests for data, to reviewing historical records. These were not nearly as effective as assembling members representing as many different departments as possible all together in one room at the same time. That is, we identified personnel from the following departments who had direct or indirect experience dealing with the ACE 41 in our example in any way:

Marketing	Engineering	Operations	Quality
Regulatory	Sales	Customer Service	Warranty
Accounting	Finance	Purchasing	The Shop

It is understandable to be reluctant to have this many people away from their normal jobs at the same time, but we found the dynamic of having personnel experienced with the ACE 41 from as many departments as possible extremely valuable.

Once the relevant personnel are assembled and understand the reason for their being together, the method that seems very effective is to ask the participants to write on index cards a problem statement in 10 words or less, say aloud the problem statement, and tape it on a wall with large open space. It is important for the participants to be active and engaged in the exercise and having a trained facilitator is essential.

After the wall is covered with index cards, the facilitator leads the participants in moving the index cards around in rows to form similar categories, as shown in Figure 7.6. This is a very organic process with the objective to have the participants "own" the problem statements and the categories they are forming. Once the rows have been formed, categories are defined, written on another index card, and placed at the top of each row. Categories that are likely to be defined are quality, health, processing, control, rework, customer, travel, communications, operations, marketing, cost, returns, transportation, and wrong materials.

The issues from the cards should be transferred to a permanent document, such as a PowerPoint document that will be used to evaluate the degree the issues are affecting the performance of the company.

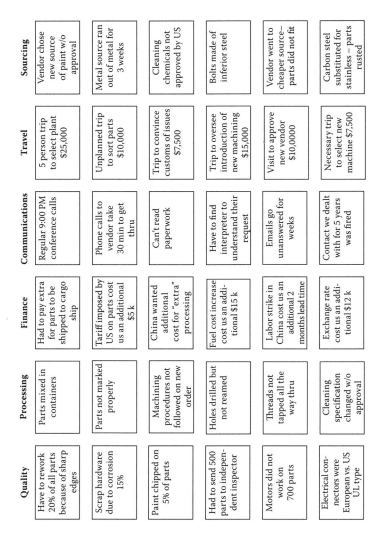

FIGURE 7.6
Intangible and hidden issues the ACE 41 is causing.

Step 5. Conduct a SWOT Analysis of Having the Product Offshored

Thus far, we have collected two financial indicators of the offshored ACE 41 and a full 360° input of the intangible and hidden issues its offshoring is causing. Remember, this is an inclusive model and gathering more information from your financial department (e.g., total cost of ownership, EBITDA, revenue per FTE, etc.) and from actual customers is encouraged.

The SWOT (strengths, weaknesses, opportunities, threats) analysis is the process, after sufficient data have been gathered, of answering the question, "What are the strengths, weaknesses, opportunities, and threats of having the ACE 41 offshored?" The SWOT is assigned to the leadership team, as they will be making a decision whether or not to proceed to phase II—exploring whether to reshore the ACE 41 or not. Answers to the SWOT questions should be well thought out and based on what the data of steps 1 through 4 say about being aligned with your vision, mission, and strategy.

For example, if your vision is "to serve our community, employees, and customers in world-class fashion," but the results of steps 2, 3, and 4 reveal that employees are spending an unusual amount of resources redoing and fixing many of the ACE 41s, or dealing unfavorably with the ACE company offshore, then a weakness or threat could be focused toward your vision.

If your mission is to "make the best ACE 41 in the world," but results of steps 2, 3, and 4 reveal that customers are dissatisfied with quality, performance, and warranties and that returned goods are over budget, then a threat to your mission might be found.

If your strategy is to "achieve a 15% reduction in product cost," and the unit cost, Velocity of Cash, and the cash conversion cycle are within limits of your financial targets, then strength might be shown toward your strategy. The goal of the SWOT analysis is to be as objective as possible based on the data discovered in steps 1 through 4.

Leadership teams are very protective of their time, so efficiency in gathering the SWOT data is critical. One method that has proven to be effective is to give a homework assignment to the leadership team, after steps 1 through 4 have been conducted, to make their own list of strengths, weaknesses, opportunities, and threats. Then the team members bring their SWOTs to a session where the entire leadership team can share their ideas and reach consensus using the index cards method similar to step 4.

A trained facilitator should lead the team to write statements on index cards first about strengths and to post them on a large-space wall. After the wall is covered with index cards, the facilitator leads the participants in moving the index cards around in rows to form similar categories. The process would continue then to weaknesses, opportunities, and, finally, threats and, after the session transfer, the SWOT data are posted to a permanent document, such as the PowerPoint one shown in Figure 7.7.

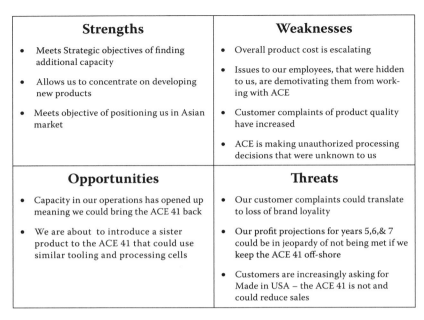

Strengths	Weaknesses
• Meets Strategic objectives of finding additional capacity • Allows us to concentrate on developing new products • Meets objective of positioning us in Asian market	• Overall product cost is escalating • Issues to our employees, that were hidden to us, are demotivating them from working with ACE • Customer complaints of product quality have increased • ACE is making unauthorized processing decisions that were unknown to us
Opportunities	**Threats**
• Capacity in our operations has opened up meaning we could bring the ACE 41 back • We are about to introduce a sister product to the ACE 41 that could use similar tooling and processing cells	• Our customer complaints could translate to loss of brand loyalty • Our profit projections for years 5,6,& 7 could be in jeopardy of not being met if we keep the ACE 41 off-shore • Customers are increasingly asking for Made in USA – the ACE 41 is not and could reduce sales

FIGURE 7.7
SWOT analysis of having the ACE 41 offshored.

Phase I, "assessment of the current state," is now complete and we are ready to continue to phase II, "select and analyze the new onshore manufacturing source." For illustrative purposes, we are assuming the information in phase I was sufficient to explore reshoring the ACE 41. As a refresher, the three-phase model is shown in Figure 7.8.

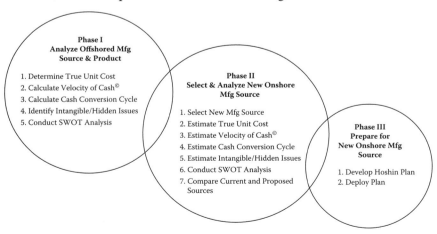

FIGURE 7.8
Reshoring Decision-Making Model.

8

Phase II: Select and Analyze the New Onshore Manufacturing Source

Motivated to overcome the issues of having the ACE 41 made offshore, the objective of phase II is to determine one or several alternatives onshore in the United States where the product can be manufactured. To keep the products separated and easier to distinguish, we will call the reshored product the USA 41. It has all the design and processing specifications that the ACE 41 has, or is supposed to have.

In phase II, you will select one or several manufacturing sources to make the USA 41 and then estimate the same elements for the USA 41 as done in phase I. A comparison will then be made between the sources and a decision to keep the ACE 41 offshored, reshore the USA 41, or some other decision. The purpose of the model, again, is to develop sufficient data to make an intelligent decision.

The steps of phase II are the following:

1. Select new manufacturing source
2. Estimate the USA 41's true unit cost
3. Estimate the USA 41's Velocity of Cash©
4. Estimate the USA 41's cash conversion cycle
5. Estimate the USA 41's intangible and hidden issues it could cause if reshored
6. Estimate the strengths, weaknesses, opportunities, and threats (SWOT) of reshoring the USA 41

STEP 1. SELECT NEW MANUFACTURING SOURCE

You are looking for a new place to make the USA 41. What are the elements you will want to consider in making a decision? Here are a few, but again, we do not presume this list to be all inclusive; the list will change—especially as time changes, which it is doing at an ever increasing rate:

- Lean methodology
- In house or outsourced
- Engineering design and manufacturing process
- Engineering and manufacturing equipment
- Materials supply
- Labor availability

Lean Methodology

Ever since the 1970s, the Toyota production system has been known to manufacturers in the United States. Some of us experienced what can be called the Deming era. W. Edwards Deming is known for introducing to the United States statistical processes for improving quality that he taught to the Japanese manufacturers during World War II reconstruction. Some US companies listened to Deming, but the Ford Motor Company benefited most from his teachings by learning his techniques of statistical process control (SPC) in manufacturing automatic transmissions. Deming and SPC were the beginnings of our introduction to Lean.

Next came the era of kaizen and manufacturing cells in the late 1980s. It was brought to the United States by past engineers and executives from Toyota who formed the consulting company Shingijutsu, led by Yoshiki Iwata. They worked only with clients who would adopt their methodologies of single piece flow, kaizen, minimal work in process, and respect for the workers. Those of us who were part of their movement and their sometimes difficult teaching method will remember Mr. Nakao yelling at us in Japanese to go to gemba to "see what is really happening on the shop floor." We did, and we learned more than any book could ever teach us about manufacturing. Kaizen and manufacturing cells took us much further toward Lean, but the Japanese were rather harsh and impatient in their teaching methods. Some US companies were resistant to their methodologies.

Then the era of Lean was introduced by James Womack, who took the Toyota production system and Americanized it with the term *Lean*. His book, *Lean Thinking,* gave a complete picture of how to connect the dots that the Shingijutsu consultants were slow to do for us. Womack made the Toyota production system easier to understand, but more importantly, he made it compelling to implement! Consultants who learned from Shingijutsu and other first-generation Toyota production system experts began teaching American manufacturers how to implement Lean in their companies. Those companies that became fully immersed in Lean showed phenomenal results, for example:

- Lead time (time from release of order to shop to product ready for sale)
  - 70%–90% reduction
- Work in process (materials that have some processing and labor toward becoming products ready for sale)
  - 80%–90% reduction
- First-time quality (parts or products inspected at the end of production line meeting quality specifications)
  - 99%–99.5%
- Labor content (total amount of labor touch time in making the product)
  - 30%–33% reduction
- Space (floor space needed to make the product)
  - 25%–50% reduction
- Invoice receipts (time from invoice issued to customer to cash placed in bank)
  - 30%–50% faster

If you decide to reshore your USA 41, you will want to apply as many Lean techniques as possible. The companies that have been successful in keeping their production in America use Lean as a way of life. Lean keeps their costs low, output fast and reliable, quality high, employees productive and happy, and customers satisfied.

Implementing Lean is a commitment that must be made by the leadership team. Lean is a journey, not a program of the month that ends when the leaders lose their enthusiasm or become discouraged.

Lean can be applied to produce your USA 41 whether it is made in house, outsourced, or a combination of both.

In House or Outsourced

Most likely, the next question to be answered is where the USA 41 will be made, in house or outsourced? If you do not have the experience, capabilities, space, or desire to manufacture the USA 41, you will be looking for an outsourced option. This will especially be true if your USA 41 is a commodity item, such as pump, motor, appliance, etc. The other considerations (i.e., manufacturing process, equipment, etc.) will have varying degrees of interest and involvement for you. However, do not make the mistake of ignoring how your USA 41 is made and the raw materials and components it is made from. You might not be any better off, and not know it, until time has passed and history of your reshored USA 41 has given you another black eye, so to speak. The lesson here is to do your homework and due diligence.

If you do have the manufacturing experience, capability, and desire to manufacture your USA 41, then, by all means, proceed onward. Choosing the in-house option will provide a great degree of control that offshoring or outsourcing does not. However, along with that is the responsibility to make good judgments on the other considerations.

Engineering Design and Manufacturing Process

When General Electric decided to reshore its water heaters from China to Louisville, Kentucky, the company took a novel approach in deciding how to manufacture it back in the United States. The manager in charge of the water heater's new life in the United States assembled a team of employees representing virtually every aspect of the water heater product: marketing, customer service, design engineering, finance, accounting, manufacturing engineering, and union shop workers. The team was asked to evaluate the offshored China-made water heater for its *functionability*—how it performed in customers' homes, its *manufacturability*—how easily it could be manufactured and assembled in the United States, and its *profitability*—how it was making money for the company.

The team found design improvements that would make the water heater perform better for homeowners, make it easier to manufacture and assemble for the shop workers, and make it cost less than when made in China. The savings are planned to be passed on to the customers; what a win–win for everyone! The customers get a better product for less cost, the company makes more money and probably sells more because of the made in America advantage, workers have jobs and are involved, and Louisville's unemployment goes down with less drain on city, state, and federal funding to the unemployed.

The lesson learned is to be creative and discover ways to reintroduce your own USA 41 to design and manufacturing. Chances are you will end up with a better product, too.

Manufacturing Equipment

Whether you are making your USA 41 in house or outsourcing its production, you will want to know the capacity and quality of the equipment being used to design and manufacture your product. In today's world, design engineering and manufacturing are becoming one. Products and components are designed in CAD (computer-aided design) and then transferred electronically to manufacturing equipment to make them. Here is a very partial list of engineering and manufacturing equipment to consider:

- CAD
  - AutoCAD
  - Autodesk
  - AllyCad
  - FreeCAD
- Welding equipment
  - MIG (metal inert gas)
  - TIG (tungsten inert gas)
  - Arc or stick
  - Robotic MIG
  - Spot or resistance
  - Gas or oxy-acetylene
- Metal removal
  - CNC center
  - Milling machine
  - Lathe
  - VTL (vertical turret lathe)
  - HBM (horizontal boring machine)
  - Drill press
  - Planer
  - Shaper
  - EDM (electrical discharge machine)
  - ECM (electrochemical machine)
- Cutting
  - Water jet

- Plasma
- Band saw
- Shear
- Abrasive wheel
- Laser
- Bending
  - Press brake
  - Folder
  - Tube bender
- Molding—plastics
  - Rotational
  - Blow
  - Injection
  - Compression
  - Extrusion
- Casting—metals
  - Die cast machine
  - Sand cast foundry
  - Powder metallurgy machine
- 3-D Printers
  - Buy
  - Lease
    - Inhouse
    - Outhouse
- Stamping
  - Coin machine
  - Press
- Grinding
  - Surface grinder
  - Cylindrical grinder
  - Hand grinder
- Coating
  - Paint gun and booth
  - Powder coat machine

This list is but a very small example of processes and equipment that might be required to manufacture your USA 41. You will need an experienced project manager to assemble a team composed of design, manufacturing, quality, supervision, shop, and finance personnel to make a determination of the manufacturing engineering and manufacturing equipment and evaluate capabilities. For example, the following is a list of general questions to ask. Of course, the specifics will change depending upon the equipment:

- Applicability
  - Will it meet our needs?
  - How will it perform compared to a different type of machine?
  - What other type of machine would you recommend?
- Availability
  - Where is it?
  - Can we see it?
  - Can we get a demo?
  - When will the model we want be available?
- Cost
  - What is the purchase cost?
  - What is the lease cost?
  - What is the operating cost?
  - What is the delivery cost?
  - What is the installation cost?
- Performance
  - What is the duty cycle of the machine?
  - How big a cut can it make in steel, aluminum, etc.?
  - What will bog it down?
- Reliability
  - What is the warranty on the machine?
  - What could cause a stoppage?
  - What could cause a breakdown?
  - Service
    - Can we get a service contract for it?
    - What companies service it?
    - What is their reputation for speed and competency?
    - What is the cost range for a service call?
  - Expendables
    - What brand and type of coolant do you recommend?
    - What brand of weld wire do you recommend?
    - What cutters and cutting tools will work best?
  - Tolerance
    - What tolerances will it hold in x, y, z axes?

- What tolerances will it hold boring?
- What tolerances will it hold milling?
- What tolerances will it hold turning?
- What tolerances will it hold threading?
- Repeatability
  - What is the repeatability in x, y, z axes?
  - What is the repeatability in boring?
  - What is the repeatability in milling?
  - What is the repeatability in turning?
  - What is the repeatability in threading?
- CAD capability
  - What CAD systems are compatible with it?
  - What CAD systems does it work best with?
  - What CAD systems should be avoided?
- Setups
  - What is the procedure for making a setup to…?
  - What tooling is necessary for making a setup to…?
  - How long does it take to make a setup to…?
- Cleanup
  - How difficult is it to remove chips?
  - How difficult is it to clean up for a new setup?
- What is the procedure for a general cleanup?

Doing due diligence will require a well thought out plan, the right people to evaluate the equipment, and time to ask the questions that will let you make the proper equipment choices. If the decision is to outsource your USA 41, for all or partial manufacturing, most of the questions still apply because they will affect the quality, cost, and delivery time of the USA 41. It is important to keep a close eye on all outsourced manufacturing to ensure that the equipment being used is yielding the best product at the best cost.

Materials Supply

You will need materials to make your USA 41. Your engineering, manufacturing, and purchasing experts will be able to identify the materials that will meet design specifications and be efficient to manufacture, at the best terms. "Best terms" means unit price, small JIT (just in time) delivery quantities, favorable payment terms, etc. Without these three experts working together, any one of the needs might not be met and your costs could get out of control.

Here are some items to consider:

- Materials source
  - Years in business
  - Reputation
  - Affiliation with professional societies
  - Quality
  - Product lead time
  - Geographic distance from you
  - Easy to work with
  - Delivery frequencies
  - Willingness to restock to your point of use versus deliver at dock
- Raw materials
  - Meet engineering specifications
  - Consistent from shipment to shipment
  - Compatible with manufacturing equipment
  - Minimal material removal (i.e., near net shape)
- Fasteners
  - Meet engineering specifications
  - Consistent from shipment to shipment
  - Delivered to point of use
  - Easy access from containers
  - Minimal wrappers and other nonessentials
- Support materials (welding supplies, cutting tools, etc.)
  - Work properly for applied use
  - Small quantities
  - Restocked to each point of use
  - Easy to access from container

The possibilities of materials are endless depending upon your engineering design and manufacturing processes for your USA 41. However, the need to be diligent about determining your supply sources is critical.

But what if you are going to outsource part or all of your USA 41? Do you have to be concerned with materials sourcing? Consider the frequently used term "GI-GO." Regardless of where your USA 41 is made, if there is garbage going in (GI) there will be garbage coming out (GO). Of course, you might be unaware of how your product is being made, but if there are inefficiencies and problems caused by poor materials, you will feel them in some way or another. For example:

- Lead times get extended
- Promised shipment dates are missed
- Costs are passed on
- Quality goes down
- Components do not fit
- Customers complain

In other words, you might have delegated some or all production of your USA 41, but you will feel the results if the materials source is substandard. Diligence is the keynote, again.

Labor Availability

Labor has become a difficult commodity to find, caused by economic and societal changes spurred on by the rush to offshore. Offshoring has changed the dynamic of supply and demand for manufacturing jobs. As manufacturing shifted from America to offshore, the need for machine operators to run machines diminished. Tool and die makers' jobs were gone because the tooling was now made offshore, too. Apprentice programs were dropped in companies because the need for skilled workers fell to a trickle. White-collar positions were affected, too. Manufacturing engineers, quality control engineers, and many other support office jobs became unnecessary. In some cases, whole companies closed their doors in America, only to become a brand name that was carried on offshore. Huffy Bicycles and Ohio Art, which made Etch A Sketch, are, for all intents and purposes, no longer American companies.

Some decades later, fewer parents are in manufacturing roles, which means their children are not exposed to the day-to-day life of growing up in a manufacturing family. Role models have shifted, career paths have changed, and kids do not have an eye toward manufacturing; as a result, manufacturing candidates are scarce.

With that being the lay of the land, the challenge is to find the skilled labor needed to make your USA 41. If you are already manufacturing products and are bringing the USA 41 back to your facility, finding skilled workers is already something you are good at. In fact, depending upon capacity issues, you might currently have the workforce you need to introduce the USA 41. If you are outsourcing, the outsourced companies will have the responsibility to find the skilled labor.

Planning for labor is something you will have to do, just like planning for design, equipment, etc. But it is more important because adding personnel to your current workforce will invariably change its culture, either for better or worse. We suggest using the following process to find and hire new machinists, machine operators, engineers, etc. The time commitment on you is minimal and the results have proven exceptional.

Step 1. Post the Position

Posting the position should include:

- Position title
- Job in broad terms
- Detailed duties
- Salary range
- Starting date
- Minimal requirements
- Desired requirements
- Any specifics

Step 2. Review and Deselect Unqualified Candidates

- Review resumés for content and appropriateness to your requirements.
- Deselect candidates that do not meet minimum requirements.
- Sort by candidates that meet both minimum and desired requirements.
- Send letter of regret to deselected candidates.

Step 3. Send a Questionnaire and Exercise to the Selected Candidates

- Questions to the candidates
  - The questionnaire should be specific to the position you are filling and to your culture:
    - Why do you want the position?
    - What is your salary history over the past (list time frame)?
    - How often did you perform (list tasks, duties, etc.) within the past (list time frame)?
    - How would you rate your proficiency at (list tasks, duties, etc.)?
    - What do you like about the position?
    - What will be challenges for you in the position?

- Give an example when you were successful with (name a scenario).
  - Give an example when you were not successful with (name a scenario) and what you learned from it.
  - Describe your work ethic.
- Exercise
  - The exercise is intended to test the skills of the candidate for the position. This may be less appropriate for positions like machine operator or welder, where practical demonstration of the skill can be observed and could be conducted the same day as Step 4, the group interview.
  - Examples of exercises sent
    - Design the manufacturing plan to produce (fictitious product with fictitious engineering drawing).
    - Design the quality plan for (fictitious product with fictitious engineering drawing).
  - Define the supply chain for (fictitious product with fictitious engineering drawing).

Step 4. Group Interview

- The setting would be the candidate and a representative sample of potential co-workers, direct supervisor, area manager, human resources manager, etc. As identified in step 3, if the candidate has demonstrated a skill such as operating a machine or welding, the group interview could be held the same day.
  - Examples of interview questions
    - "Tell us about yourself."
    - "How do you think you would fit in here?"
    - "We have a few questions about the exercise you took" or
    - "We have a few questions about how you (...ran the machine...performed the setup...programmed the controller...welded the...)."
    - "Now that we have asked you these questions, what questions do you have of us?"
    - "Thank you for coming in today. We will let you know of our decision."

This process, with its thoroughness and inclusivity of potential co-workers and supervisors, will always yield a good hiring decision and provide you with the labor, whether blue collar or white collar, to manufacture your USA 41.

Summary

To wrap it up, the effort to bring your own USA 41 back to American soil will depend on several factors:

- Your current experience in direct or outsourcing manufacturing
- The complexity and volume of your USA 41
- The pool of labor to design, source materials, and manufacture your USA 41
- The availability and skill of personnel to lead the effort to reshore your USA 41

The next step in phase II is to estimate the USA 41's true unit cost.

STEP 2. ESTIMATE THE ONSHORED PRODUCT'S TRUE UNIT COST

To illustrate the process of estimating the USA 41's true unit cost, we will make some assumptions:

- Lean manufacturing, administrative, and technical processes will be applied.
  - Lean manufacturing processes
    - Manufacturing cells
    - JIT with kanban
    - Materials presented to cell with water spider
    - Intelligent automation with jidoka
    - Mistake proofing built in with poka-yoke
    - Single piece flow
    - Minimal WIP (work in process)
    - Minimal FGI (finished goods inventory)
  - Lean administrative/technical processes

- Order entry
- CAD
- Engineering change notices
- Purchase orders
- Invoicing
- Remittance to bank

- Production is within 10 to 60 minutes away from the company's resources and personnel to allow the following departments to:
  - *Marketing:* ensure product meets customer expectations and marketing objectives.
  - *Engineering:* ensure product is meeting engineering requirements.
  - *Operations:* make in-house manufacturing decision/outsource decision but in close proximity.
  - *Quality:* ensure that product is meeting engineering and manufacturing requirements.
  - *Regulatory:* ensure that product is meeting regulatory requirements.
  - *Sales:* ensure that product availability meets customer expectations.
  - *Customer Service:* respond quickly to customer complaints.
  - *Warranty:* validate warranty claims.
  - *Accounting:* determine cost metrics for quick and accurate decision making.
  - *Controller:* determine cost reduction opportunities.
  - *Finance:* assess capital opportunities.
  - *Purchasing:* validate materials input and purchasing opportunities.
- Sales (identical to ACE 41)
  - Weekly sales: 500 units
  - Selling price: $15.00 each
  - Receivable terms: 4 weeks
- Purchasing terms
  - Raw materials unit cost: $2.50 each
  - Order quantity: 1,500 units
  - Lead time: 3 weeks
  - Payment terms: 4 weeks
- Cost before receiving parts
  - Trucking costs to bring materials locally to production site
    - $75.00 per order

- Cost after receiving parts and during manufacturing
  - Unloading
    - $50.00 per order 100% all parts
  - Handling
    - $375.00 per order 100% all parts
  - Machining
    - $7,500.00 per order 100% all parts @ $5.00 per part
  - Assembly
    - $3,750.00 per order 100% all parts @ $2.50 per part
  - Paint
    - $750.00 per order 100% all parts @ $0.50 per part
  - Inspection
    - $112.50 per order 10% all parts @ $0.75 per part
      - Note: Inspection reduced to 10% via Lean manufacturing processes (e.g., built-in inspection during manufacturing)
  - Rework
    - $112.50 per order 5% all parts @ $1.50 per part
      - Note: Rework reduced to 5% via Lean manufacturing processes (e.g., mistake proofing during manufacturing and close proximity to company personnel to solve problems quickly)
  - Scrap
    - $225.00 per order 1% all parts @ $15.00 per part
      - Note: Scrap reduced to 1% via Lean manufacturing processes (e.g., mistake proofing during manufacturing and close proximity to company personnel to solve problems quickly)
  - Storage
    - $50.00 per order 100% all parts

This information is shown in tabular form in Tables 8.1 and 8.2. The true unit cost of the USA 41 is tabulated in Table 8.3. The estimated true unit costs of the USA 41 and ACE 41 are shown in Table 8.4.

TABLE 8.1

Sales Reshoring Estimates—USA 41

Weekly sales	500 ACE 41s
Selling price	$15.00 per ACE 41
Terms	4 wks. payment after placing order

TABLE 8.2

Purchasing Reshoring Estimates—USA 41

Purchase price per unit—raw material	$2.50
Order quantity	1500
Lead time of parts	3 wks.
Payment terms	4 wks.

TABLE 8.3

True Unit Cost (Estimated)—USA 41

Item	Cost per Order	% of Parts	Cost per Part	Avg. Cost per Part
Cost *before* receiving parts				
Truck transportation	$75.00	100%	$0.05	$0.05
Additional cost per part				**$0.05**
Cost *after* receiving parts and during manufacturing				
Unload	$50.00	100%	$0.033	$0.033
Handling	$375.00	100%	$0.25	$0.250
Machining	$7500.00	100%	$5.00	$5.000
Assembly	$3750.00	100%	$2.50	$2.500
Paint	$750.00	100%	$0.50	$0.500
Inspection	$112.50	10%	$0.75	$0.075
Rework	$112.50	5%	$1.50	$0.075
Scrap	$225.00	1%	$15.00	$0.15
Storage	$50.00	100%	$0.033	$0.033
Additional cost per part				**$8.617**
True unit cost—estimated				
Purchased price per part raw material				$2.500
Additional cost per part				
Before receiving parts				$0.050
After receiving parts				$8.617
True unit cost—estimated				**$11.167**

Notes: 1,500 parts each shipment. Purchase price: $2.50 per part raw material.

TABLE 8.4

Estimated Unit Cost—USA 41 and True Unit Cost—ACE 41

ACE 41	$11.35
US 41	$11.17

This is a sign that reshoring the ACE 41 to the United States might be a good investment, but we need to collect more data by following our Reshoring Decision-Making Model© with step 3, estimating the USA 41's Velocity of Cash©.

STEP 3. ESTIMATE THE ONSHORED PRODUCT'S VELOCITY OF CASH

A spreadsheet, shown in Figure 8.1, tracks the activity of the reshored USA 41 using the estimates made for sales and purchasing, costs before receiving raw materials, and costs afterward. A graph of cumulative profit is also shown for the USA 41 in Figure 8.2 compared to the offshored ACE 41 in Figure 8.3.

Using the same time periods for the USA 41 as for the ACE 41 and determining the cumulative profits, the Velocity of Cash for the USA 41 is calculated in Table 8.5.

Similarly to true unit cost, both products are making money for the company at the same rate at the 480-day mark, which was chosen to allow the ACE 41s to come out of the red. However, at the 4,400-day mark, the cumulative profits for the two products are quite different (as shown in Table 8.6). This is caused by the early weeks of nonprofitability for the offshored ACE 41.

We will see if there are any differences in the cash conversion cycle for USA 41 when we move to step 4 in the model.

STEP 4. ESTIMATE THE ONSHORED PRODUCT'S CASH CONVERSION CYCLE

Using the assumptions made for the reshored USA 41 and reading the spreadsheet of the estimated USA 41's activity, its cash conversion cycle can be determined. The data are arranged in Table 8.7 as they were for the ACE 41.

Cash conversion results for the USA 41 are shown in Table 8.8. We can compare the cash conversion cycle for both the offshored ACE 41 and the estimated reshored USA 41, as shown in Table 8.9. Remember that the cash conversion cycle is a measurement of how *quickly* our products are making money for us, the 0 to 60 mph analogy.

Week	Order Parts	Inventory		Payables			Extra Cost		Sales				Profit	
		Rcv Inv	Net Inv Quan	Acc Pay Booked	Acc Pay Paid	Acc Pay Balance	Before Receiving Parts	After Receiving Parts	Weekly Sales	Acc Rcv Booked	Acc Rcv Rcv'd	Acc Rcv Cumulative	Profit Daily	Profit Cum
0	#1												$0	$0
1													$0	$0
2													$0	$0
3	#2	1500	1,500	$3,750		3,750	Truck 75.00	Total $12,925	500	$7,500	0	7,500	−$13,000	−$13,000
4			1,000	$0		3,750			500	$7,500	0	15,000	$0	−$13,000
5			500	$0	0	3,750			500	$7,500	0	22,500	$0	−$13,000
6	#3	1500	1,500	$3,750	0	7,500	Truck 75.00	Total $12,925	500	$7,500	7,500	30,000	−$13,000	−$26,000
7			1,000	$0	0	3,750			500	$7,500	7,500	30,000	−$3,750	−$29,750
8			500	$0	3,750	3,750			500	$7,500	7,500	30,000	$7,500	−$22,250
9	#4	1500	1,500	$3,750	0	7,500	Truck 75.00	Total $12,925	500	$7,500	7,500	30,000	−$5,500	−$27,750
10			1,000	$0	0	3,750			500	$7,500	7,500	30,000	$3,750	−$24,000
11			500	$0	3,750	3,750			500	$7,500	7,500	30,000	$7,500	−$16,500
12	#5	1500	1,500	$3,750	0	7,500	Truck 75.00	Total $12,925	500	$7,500	7,500	30,000	−$5,500	−$22,000
13			1,000	$0	0	3,750			500	$7,500	7,500	30,000	$3,750	−$18,250
14			500	$0	3,750	3,750			500	$7,500	7,500	30,000	$7,500	−$10,750
15	#6	1500	1,500	$3,750	0	7,500	Truck 75.00	Total $12,925	500	$7,500	7,500	30,000	−$5,500	−$16,250
16			1,000	$0	0	3,750			500	$7,500	7,500	30,000	$3,750	−$12,500
17			500	$0	3,750	3,750			500	$7,500	7,500	30,000	$7,500	−$5,000
18	#7	1500	1,500	$3,750	0	7,500	Truck 75.00	Total $12,925	500	$7,500	7,500	30,000	−$5,500	−$10,500
19			1,000	$0	0	3,750			500	$7,500	7,500	30,000	$3,750	−$6,750
20			500	$0	3,750	3,750			500	$7,500	7,500	30,000	$7,500	$750
21	#8	1500	1,500	$3,750	0	7,500	Truck 75.00	Total $12,925	500	$7,500	7,500	30,000	−$5,500	−$4,750
22			1,000	$0	0	3,750			500	$7,500	7,500	30,000	$3,750	−$1,000
23			500	$0	3,750	3,750			500	$7,500	7,500	30,000	$7,50	$6,500
24	#9	1500	1,500	$3,750	0	7,500	Truck 75.00	Total $12,925	500	$7,500	7,500	30,000	−$5,500	$1,000
25			1,000	$0	0	3,750			500	$7,500	7,500	30,000	$3,750	$4,750
26			500	$0	3,750	3,750			500	$7,500	7,500	30,000	$7,500	$12,250
27	#10	1500	1,500	$3,750	0	7,500	Truck 75.00	Total $12,925	500	$7,500	7,500	30,000	−$5,500	$6,750
28			1,000	$0	3,750	3,750			500	$7,500	7,500	30,000	$3,750	$10,500

FIGURE 8.1

Reshored USA 41 activity. (Continued)

Week	Order Parts	Inventory		Payables			Extra Cost				Sales				Profit	
		Rcv Inv	Net Inv Quan	Acc Pay Booked	Acc Pay Paid	Acc Pay Balance	Before Receiving Parts		After Receiving Parts		Weekly Sales	Acc Rcv Booked	Acc Rcv Rcv'd	Acc Rcv Cumulative	Profit Daily	Profit Cum
29			500	$0	0	3,750					500	$7,500	7,500	30,000	$7,500	$18,000
30	#11	1500	1,500	$3,750	3,750	7,500	Truck	75.00	Total	$12,925	500	$7,500	7,500	30,000	-$5,500	$12,500
31			1,000	$0	0	3,750					500	$7,500	7,500	30,000	$3,750	$16,250
32			500	$0	0	3,750					500	$7,500	7,500	30,000	$7,500	$23,750
33	#12	1500	1,500	$3,750	3,750	7,500	Truck	75.00	Total	$12,925	500	$7,500	7,500	30,000	-$5,500	$18,250
34			1,000	$0	0	3,750					500	$7,500	7,500	30,000	$3,750	$22,000
35			500	$0	0	3,750					500	$7,500	7,500	30,000	$7,500	$29,500
36	#13	1500	1,500	$3,750	3,750	7,500	Truck	75.00	Total	$12,925	500	$7,500	7,500	30,000	-$5,500	$24,000
37			1,000	$0	0	3,750					500	$7,500	7,500	30,000	$3,750	$27,750
38			500	$0	0	3,750					500	$7,500	7,500	30,000	$7,500	$35,250
39	#14	1500	1,500	$3,750	3,750	7,500	Truck	75.00	Total	$12,925	500	$7,500	7,500	30,000	-$5,500	$29,750
40			1,000	$0	0	3,750					500	$7,500	7,500	30,000	$3,750	$33,500
41			500	$0	0	3,750					500	$7,500	7,500	30,000	$7,500	$41,000
42	#15	1500	1,500	$3,750	3,750	7,500	Truck	75.00	Total	$12,925	500	$7,500	7,500	30,000	-$5,500	$35,500
43			1,000	$0	0	3,750					500	$7,500	7,500	30,000	$3,750	$39,250
44			500	$0	0	3,750					500	$7,500	7,500	30,000	$7,500	$46,750
45	#16	1500	1,500	$3,750	3,750	7,500	Truck	75.00	Total	$12,925	500	$7,500	7,500	30,000	-$5,500	$41,250
46			1,000	$0	0	3,750					500	$7,500	7,500	30,000	$3,750	$45,000
47			500	$0	0	3,750					500	$7,500	7,500	30,000	$7,500	$52,500
48	#17	1500	1,500	$3,750	3,750	7,500	Truck	75.00	Total	$12,925	500	$7,500	7,500	30,000	-$5,500	$47,000
49			1,000	$0	0	3,750					500	$7,500	7,500	30,000	$3,750	$50,750
50			500	$0	0	3,750					500	$7,500	7,500	30,000	$7,500	$58,250
51	#18	1500	1,500	$3,750	3,750	7,500	Truck	75.00	Total	$12,925	500	$7,500	7,500	30,000	-$5,500	$52,750
52			1,000	$0	0	3,750					500	$7,500	7,500	30,000	$3,750	$56,500
53			500	$0	0	3,750					500	$7,500	7,500	30,000	$7,500	$64,000
54	#19	1500	1,500	$3,750	3,750	7,500	Truck	75.00	Total	$12,925	500	$7,500	7,500	30,000	-$5,500	$58,500
55			1,000	$0	0	3,750					500	$7,500	7,500	30,000	$3,750	$62,250
56			500	$0	0	3,750					500	$7,500	7,500	30,000	$7,500	$69,750
57	#20	1500	1,500	$3,750	3,750	7,500	Truck	75.00	Total	$12,925	500	$7,500	7,500	30,000	-$5,500	$64,250
58			1,000	$0	0	3,750					500	$7,500	7,500	30,000	$3,750	$68,000
59			500	$0	0	3,750					500	$7,500	7,500	30,000	$7,500	$75,500
60	#21	1500	1,500	$3,750	3,750	7,500	Truck	75.00	Total	$12,925	500	$7,500	7,500	30,000	-$5,500	$70,000
61			1,000	$0	0	3,750					500	$7,500	7,500	30,000	$3,750	$73,750
62			500	$0	0	3,750					500	$7,500	7,500	30,000	$7,500	$81,250

FIGURE 8.1 (CONTINUED)
Reshored USA 41 activity.

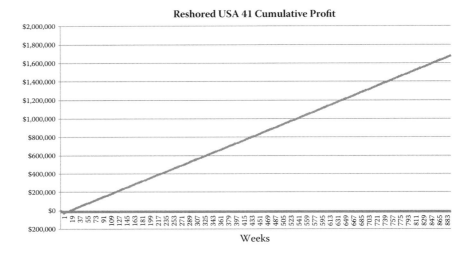

FIGURE 8.2
Reshored USA 41 cumulative profit.

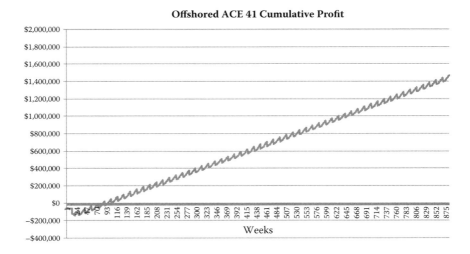

FIGURE 8.3
Offshored ACE 41 cumulative profit.

TABLE 8.5

Velocity of Cash Calculation—USA 41

Velocity of cash reshored USA 41	=	(Cum. profit @ time period 2 – Cum. profit @ time period 1)
		(Time period 2 – Time period 1)

Cum. profit @ time period 2	=	$1,643,500	Time period 2	=	Day 4,400
Cum. profit @ time period 1	=	$ 875,000	Time period 1	=	Day 2,400
Subtracting 1 from 2	=	$ 768,500			2,000 Days

Velocity of cash reshored USA 41	=	$786, 500
		2,000 Days
		$384.25 per Day

TABLE 8.6

Cumulative Profit Comparison of ACE 41 and USA 41 at Day 4400

Product	Cumulative Profit
USA 41	$1,643,500
ACE 41	$1,455,782
Cumulative profit increase for USA 41	$187,718 = 13% increase

TABLE 8.7

Cash Conversion Calculation—USA 41

Avg. receivable days	=	Avg. receivables for the quarter ($)	÷	Sales per day ($)
	=	$30,000	÷	$7,500 per wk. ÷ 5 days per wk. = $1,500 per day
Avg. receivable days	=		**20.00 Days**	
Avg. payable days	=	Avg. payables for the quarter ($)	÷	Purchases per day ($)
	=	$4,903.85	÷	1,500 units per order × $2.50 per unit ÷ 3 wks. per order ÷ 5 days per wk. = $250 per day
Avg. payable days	=		**19.62 Days**	
Avg. inventory days	=	Avg. inventory for the quarter ($)	÷	Cost of goods sold per day ($)
	=	1,000 avg. units per wk. × $11.167 total cost per unit = $11,167.00	÷	500 units per wk. × $11.167 total cost per unit ÷ 5 days per wk. = $1,116.70 per day
Avg. inventory days	=		**10.00 Days**	

TABLE 8.8

Cash Conversion Cycle Results—USA 41

Avg. Receivable Days	–	Avg. Payable Days	+	Avg. Inventory Days	=	Cash Conversion Cycle Days
20.00	–	19.62	+	10.00	=	10.38

TABLE 8.9

Comparison Cash Conversion Cycle USA 41 and ACE 41

Product	Cash Conversion Cycle
ACE 41	75.00 Days
USA 41	10.38 Days
Cash conversion cycle; reduction in time for USA 41	64.62 Days = 86% more quickly

Summarizing the three quantitative factors, perhaps we can think about it in the following way:

1. The ACE 41 and USA 41 cost about the same, with the USA 41 estimated at a slightly less total unit cost.
   a. ACE 41: $11.35/unit
   b. USA 41: $11.17/unit (estimated)

2. The ACE 41 and USA 41 have about the same constant Velocity of Cash in making money.
   a. ACE 41: $384.64/day
   b. USA 41: $384.25/day (estimated)

3. The USA 41 is estimated to generate 13% more cumulative profit than the ACE 41 by day 4,400.
   a. USA 41: $1,643,500 (estimated)
   b. ACE 41: $1,455,782

4. The USA 41 is estimated to turn our money 86% more quickly than the ACE 41.
   a. ACE 41: 75.00 days
   b. USA 41: 10.38 days (estimated)

This is valuable information. We now need to proceed to the next step of phase II.

STEP 5. ESTIMATE THE INTANGIBLE AND HIDDEN ISSUES OF RESHORING THE PRODUCT

The USA 41 is not being made in the United States yet, and since the plan to reshore it will encompass many elements inside and outside the company, we will want to bring together all those representatives to help identify the intangible and hidden issues that might occur with the USA 41 during and after its reshoring. The representatives inside the company include:

Marketing	Engineering	Operations	Quality
Regulatory	Sales	Customer Service	Warranty
Accounting	Finance	Purchasing	The shop

We have chosen to include the following representatives from outside our company:

Customers	Field reps	Distributors
Building contractors	Machinery reps	Local tax official
Chamber of commerce rep	Supply chain reps	

Using the same group process as with the ACE 41, the team arrived at the issues shown in Figure 8.4.

The majority of the issues are about the process of reshoring the USA 41 and the concern of where the team members will find the time to get everything done. Finance has concerns that the exchange rates for the yuan and dollar remain favorable regarding the reshoring decision. Time will tell if other issues surface, but at this time we have mostly issues of making the reshoring happen. The next step is to conduct a SWOT analysis of reshoring the USA 41.

STEP 6. CONDUCT A SWOT ANALYSIS OF HAVING THE PRODUCT RESHORED

The leadership team has gathered a cornucopia of information about the USA 41. Here is a quick summary:

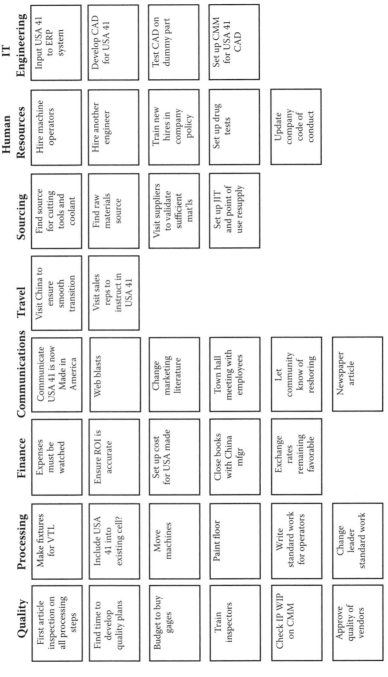

FIGURE 8.4
Intangible and hidden issues that the USA 41 might cause.

- Step 1: Selecting the new manufacturing location, considering:
  - Applying Lean methodology to be competitive with the ACE in China
  - Manufacturing in house or outsourcing
  - Having or acquiring the necessary manufacturing and processing equipment
  - Redesigning the USA 41 with a team approach
  - Determining the material supply chain
  - Designing a plan to hire office, technical, and shop labor

- Step 2: Estimating the true unit cost of $11.17, which is $0.18 lower than the ACE 41, considering:
  - Manufacturing location is close to company support personnel (e.g., Engineering, Accounting, Marketing, and Purchasing permitting rapid response to issues, problems, and requests). The net effect is very low rework and scrap.
  - Smaller order quantities of raw materials mitigate the issue of defects found in incoming quality.

- Step 3: Estimating the USA 41 will make money at a Velocity of Cash of $384.25 per day, which is virtually identical to the ACE 41, considering:
  - Calculating the estimated cumulative profit of $768,500 over a period of 400 weeks
  - Discovering that the estimated cumulative profit for the USA 41 is $187,718 greater than the ACE 41 at week 880, or 16.9 years

- Step 4: Estimating the 0 to 60 time cash conversion cycle of the USA 41 at 10.38 days, which is 86% more quickly than the 75 days of the ACE 41, considering:
  - Better, longer payment terms for raw material
  - Smaller order quantities
  - More frequent orders

- Step 5: Estimating the hidden and intangible costs of the USA 41, considering:
  - What is known about manufacturing in America
  - Experience of setting up a new product for manufacturing
  - Customer and other adjunct input

Strengths	Weaknesses
• Production close to company support personnel gives more control over process adherence & quality control • Smaller order quantities mitigates threat of non-conforming in-coming materials • Favorable purchasing terms speeds up Cash Conversion Cycle by 86% • Customers have been asking for "Made in America" for a long time	• We will be "closing our door" of opportunity in China • Putting all our eggs in US manufacturing setting
Opportunities	**Threats**
• New marketing for "Made in America" • Redesign USA 41 for DMFA* for lower cost and ease of manufacture • Redesign USA 41 for better functionality by end user • Implement Lean across entire product line * Design for Manufacturability and Assembly	• Transition from China to US will consume resources of time, people, and money • Finding reliable supply chain • Hiring scarce human resources, e.g. skilled machine operators, tool makers

FIGURE 8.5
SWOT analysis of having the USA 41 reshored.

Armed with the aforementioned information, the leadership team can now conduct its SWOT analysis. Figure 8.5 shows what a leadership team might generate.

STEP 7. COMPARE THE CURRENT AND PROPOSED SOURCES

We are now at the culmination of assimilating the vast amount of data generated to make the decision to reshore or not. Our research has shown that it is important to continue applying the 360° approach in making the decision, involving the team that has been developing the data for the ACE 41 and USA 41. Inclusion not only enhances the quality of the decision, but also develops buy-in of the team. The issue now is to provide a

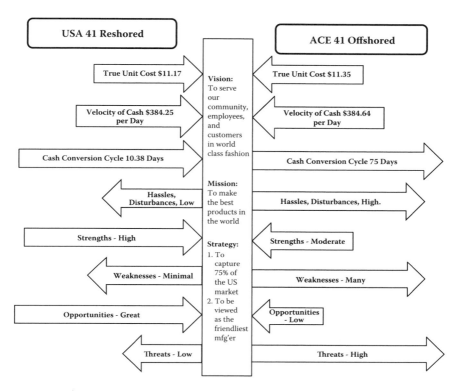

FIGURE 8.6
Comparison of reshoring versus offshoring.

comparison method that presents the data in a way that is accurate, easy to see, meaningful, and displayed to avoid biases, as shown in Figure 8.6.

The method we have developed is one in which the vision, mission, and strategy of the company are centered in the diagram and on one side are the results of the data for the reshoring effort expressed by arrows directed toward or away from the vision, mission, and strategy. The arrows are of varying lengths, which express the degree of support or opposition to achieving the vision, mission, and strategy. On the other side are the data for the existing offshoring expressed in magnitude and direction of supporting or opposing the vision, mission, and strategy. The model can be enhanced by assigning weights and values to each arrow, but they have been omitted for the sake of simplicity in expressing the model. The approach is to involve the team in constructing the model with the direction and lengths of the arrows so that everyone has a stake in its creation and thus develops ownership. This contributes to arriving at a decision through dialogue, discussion, and discovery.

From the creation of the model and its ensuing discussion, a proposal can be made that the team can further dialogue until a decision is achieved. From the model shown, we will assume the leadership team has made the decision to reshore the ACE 41 back to the United States. The task at hand, then, is to lay out the plan to make the reshoring happen; this takes us to phase III of the Reshoring Decision-Making Model, "prepare for reshoring."

9

Phase III: Prepare for Reshoring

PHASE III: PREPARE FOR THE NEW ONSHORE MANUFACTURING SOURCE

Phase III involves making your decision to reshore your USA 41 a reality (Figure 9.1) and has two steps:

1. Develop the hoshin plan to reshore.
2. Deploy the plan.

Develop the Hoshin Plan to Reshore

Hoshin is a strategic planning process, also known as hoshin kanri, policy deployment, and strategy deployment, developed by Kaoru Ishikawa in the 1950s. Hoshin is a powerful methodology to engage the entire organization in achieving what are called breakthrough objectives, or simply BTOs. Jim Collins, in his book, *Built to Last,* called BTOs "big hairy audacious goals," or B-HAGs. You can choose Collins's or Ishikawa's terminology and methodology or another one, depending upon your experiences and culture. We will demonstrate Ishikawa's hoshin planning methodology simply because it has proven to be very successful in our practice over 20 years working with both Fortune 500 companies and small manufacturing and nonmanufacturing organizations. The steps are straightforward and simple to execute per the hoshin planning model shown in Figure 9.2.

The first step in hoshin is to state what we want to accomplish in succinct terms in the form of a BTO. In our case, we want to bring the USA 41 back to America. Assuming it was decided that we want to bring the USA 41 back to America and reshore it in 2 years, our BTO could simply be, "reshore the USA 41 in 2 years." Even though it may sound like an exercise in simplicity

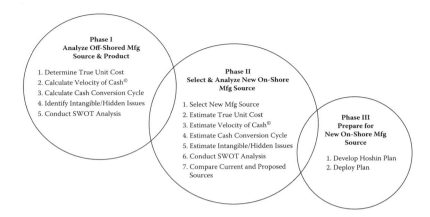

FIGURE 9.1
Reshoring Decision-Making Model©.

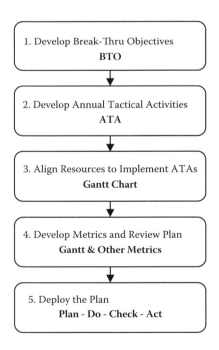

FIGURE 9.2
Hoshin planning model.

and perhaps unnecessary, the BTO provides a constant focus for the leadership team and is a means of communicating to the entire organization that reshoring the USA 41 is an important project for the company.

Next we determine what must be accomplished to support the BTO; these are called annual tactical activities, or ATAs. Our 2-year strategy is the BTO, and the annual tactical activities are the actions required to meet the strategy. We work in time frames of 1 year because, as we work toward our BTO, things may (will) change in our company, the market, our staff, or the world and we may need to adjust our tactical activities. Bringing together the leadership team and key members associated with the USA 41 will help us identify the tactical activities that must be done to reshore the USA 41.

As the ATAs are identified, a member of the leadership team is assigned responsibility for leading each ATA. The assignment of ATAs is necessary to keep track of them and their progress during the next year. The BTO and ATAs are shown in Figure 9.3.

We next must align the ATAs with resources of people, time, and money. It might be an oversimplification to say that resources are needed to make things happen, but ensuring that adequate resources are available is often overlooked. Perhaps the most visual way of aligning resources to the ATAs is to develop a project chart fashioned in the method that Henry Gantt developed over 100 years ago. Commonly called "project charts," they are simple to develop and use. Figure 9.4 shows the project chart that will be used to track the progress of our ATAs in support of our BTO—to reshore the USA 41 in 2 years.

From the partial project chart you can see that each ATA has its leader, an expected completion date for the task, estimated hours to complete the task, and estimated costs. Completing the chart can be a sobering task as people begin to think about the extra time they will have to devote. This is also true for the dollars that will be expended to bring the USA 41 back to America. Expenses and time expectations are reasons for pushing the time to 2 years. However, it will be your choice—again, depending upon your resources of time, money, and personnel—how quickly you will bring your own USA 41 back home.

Other considerations to take into account are the activities out of your control. For example, if you require tooling to be made by an outside firm or if you are buying used machinery that must be refurbished or rewired by a machinery company to meet your application, you will have to get your requests in their queue to meet the deadlines you set for your reshoring effort.

Break Thru Objective
We Will Reshore the USA 41 in 2 Years
Annual Tactical Activities — Year 1

ATA 1 Purchasing		ATA 1 Leader: Adam Smith, Purchasing mgr.
	ATA 1.1	Make preparations to place materials orders
	ATA 1.2	Alert existing sources and/or find new alternate sources
	ATA 1.3	Determine lead times for materials
	ATA 1.4	Negotiate payment terms with suppliers
ATA 2 Operations		**ATA 2 Leader: Tom Jones, Operations mgr.**
	ATA 2.1	Identify where to make the USA 41 in the shop
	ATA 2.2	Ensure machine capacity, tooling supply
	ATA 2.3	Add production control, supervision, as necessary
	ATA 2.4	Hire and/or train operators
	ATA 2.5	Close down China operations
ATA 3 Quality		**ATA 3 Leader: Susan Wilson, Quality mgr.**
	ATA 3.1	Write quality plan
	ATA 3.2	Ensure gauging is in place
	ATA 3.3	Train inspector and operators
ATA 4 HR		**ATA 4 Leader: Gene Mason, HR mgr.**
	ATA 4.1	Hire machine operators and assemblers as needed
	ATA 4.2	Hire production control, supervision, etc. as needed
ATA 5 Marketing		**ATA 5 Leader: Bill Dawes, Marketing mgr.**
	ATA 5.1	Launch "Remade in America" campaign
	ATA 5.2	Modify website
ATA 6 Sales		**ATA 6 Leader: Harry Lincoln, Sales mgr.**
	ATA 6.1	Train inside and outside company sales personnel
	ATA 6.2	Train sales reps and distributors
ATA 7 Compliance		**ATA 7 Leader: Alice Norton, Compliance mgr.**
	ATA 7.1	Modify compliance manual
	ATA 7.2	Notify compliance agencies
ATA 8 Info Tech		**ATA 8 Leader: Carl Simpson, IT mgr.**
	ATA 8.1	Modify ERP system as needed
ATA 9 Accounting		**ATA 9 Leader: Marie Baxter, Accounting mgr.**
	ATA 9.1	Modify cost accounting sheets as needed
	ATA 9.2	Modify budget and forecasts as needed
ATA 10 Leadership		**ATA 10 Leader: Doris Dayton, HR mgr.**
	ATA 10.1	Communicate BTO and ATAs to all employees
	ATA 10.2	Review Lean system and modify as necessary

FIGURE 9.3
BTO and ATAs.

ATA	Action	Person	Est Cost	Est Time	Completion Date				
					Jan	Feb	Mar	Apr	May
ATA 1	**Purchasing**	**Adam**	–	**300 hr**					
ATA 1.1	Make preparations to place materials orders	Jill	–	25 hr					3-May
ATA 1.2	Alert existing sources and/or find new alternate sources	Susan	–	100 hr			3-Mar		
ATA 1.3	Determine lead times for materials	Tim	–	25 hr				3-Apr	
ATA 1.4	Negotiate payment terms with suppliers	Denny	–	150 hr					3-May
ATA 2	**Operations**	**Tom**	**$145,000**	**350 hr**					
ATA 2.1	Identify where to make the US 41 in the shop	Ralph	–	50 hr					4-May
ATA 2.2	Ensure machine capacity, tooling supply	Andrew	$20,000	100 hr					
ATA 2.3	Add production control, supervision, as necessary	Penny	–	50 hr					
ATA 2.4	Hire and/or train operators	Carla	$75,000	50 hr					
ATA 2.5	Close down China operations	Wes	$50,000	100 hr					
ATA 3	**Quality**	**Susan**	–	**100 hr**					
ATA 3.1	Write quality plan	Dan	–	40 hr			6-Mar		
ATA 3.2	Ensure gauging is in place	Marc	–	20 hr					3-May
ATA 3.3	Train inspector and operators	Bryan	–	40 hr					
ATA 4	**Human Resources**	**Gene**	–	**100 hr**					
ATA 4.1	Hire machine operators and assemblers as needed	Max	–	50 hr					
ATA 4.2	Hire production control, supervision, etc. as needed	Terry	–	50 hr					
ATA 5	**Marketing**	**Bill**	**$10,000**	**150 hr**					
ATA 5.1	Launch "Re-Made in America" campaign	Nancy	$10,000	100 hr				2-Apr	
ATA 5.2	Modify website	Lynne	–	50 hr					5-May
ATA 6	**Sales**	**Harry**	–	**80 hr**					
ATA 6.1	Alert inside & outside company sales personnel	Chuck	–	40 hr					8-May
ATA 6.2	Alert sales reps and distributors	Andrew	–	40 hr					9-May

FIGURE 9.4
Project chart (partial).

Deploy the Hoshin Plan

Deploying the plan is a cascading process. The leadership team meets monthly to review the progress being made on each ATA with the persons assigned leadership responsibilities for the ATAs. For example, ATA 1, Purchasing, has been assigned to Adam, ATA 2, Operations, has been assigned to Tom, and so on. They will meet weekly with their personnel to ensure that the ATAs receive the attention needed for completion.

Our research has shown that visual aids, when displayed in prominent locations, are very effective in encouraging those who have responsibility for completing tasks to meet their commitments, especially when status symbols are shown by their names as shown in Figure 9.5.

To prepare for the monthly meeting, each person assigned to lead an ATA meets with his or her personnel weekly to track progress. For example, Adam meets with Jill, who has responsibility for ATA 1.1, Susan (ATA 1.2), Tim (ATA 1.3), and Denny (ATA 1.4).

To ensure progress is being made it is recommended to use a model similar to the continuous improvement model shown in Figure 9.6, which W. Edwards Deming and Walter Shewhart developed in the mid-1990s.

Using the plan–do–check–act (PDCA) model, Adam will ask for substantiating data that show that progress is being made. If progress has not been made, Adam will begin a dialogue with each of his people to develop a "get well" plan to catch up, ensuring the completion dates are met. The plan is implemented ("do"), and at the next meeting the plan is "checked" to determine if the corrective action is working; if not, the plan is "acted" upon to develop a new or revised plan. Persons who have outside resources implementing sections of their ATAs should not hesitate to apply the principles of PDCA. However, it is advised to educate outside persons with the PDCA model and its benefits of helping them meet completion dates to which they have made commitments.

If completion dates are missed, the reasons will most likely be that sufficient resources of people, time, or money were not applied. As obvious as that sounds, those resources will have to come from somewhere when dates are missed. Being prepared to shore up resources is a word to the wise. The Boy Scout motto here is very appropriate: "Be Prepared!" We are speaking especially to the leadership team. It is your responsibility to make sure that the journey continues to finality once all parties are committed, resource constraints have been shored up, budgets have been prepared, and review processes have started. Of course, if you have led change projects before, you know this, but a reminder never hurts.

ATA	Action		Person	Est Cost	Est Time	Completion Date
ATA 1	**Purchasing**	☺	**Adam**	–	**300 hr**	
ATA 1.1	Make preparations to place orders materials		Jill	–	25 hr	
ATA 1.2	Alert existing sources and/or find new alternate sources		Susan	–	100 hr	3-May
ATA 1.3	Determine lead times for materials		Tim	–	25 hr	3-Mar
ATA 1.4	Negotiate payment terms with suppliers		Denny	–	150 hr	1-Apr
ATA 2	**Operations**	⊗	**Tom**	**$145,000**	**350 hr**	
ATA 2.1	Identify where to make the US 41 in the shop		Ralph	–	50 hr	4-May
ATA 2.2	Ensure machine capacity, tooling, supply		Andrew	$20,000	100 hr	
ATA 2.3	Add production control, supervision, as necessary		Penny	–	50 hr	
ATA 2.4	Hire and/or train operators		Carla	$75,000	50 hr	
ATA 2.5	Close down China operations		Wes	$50,000	100 hr	
ATA 3	**Quality**	☺	**Susan**	–	**100 hr**	
ATA 3.1	Write quality plan		Dan	–	40 hr	6-Mar
ATA 3.2	Ensure gauging is in place		Marc	–	20 hr	3-Mar
ATA 3.3	Train inspector and operators		Bryan	–	40 hr	
ATA 4	**Human Resources**	☺	**Gene**	–	**100 hr**	
ATA 4.1	Hire machine operators and assemblers as needed		Max	–	50 hr	
ATA 4.2	Hire production control, supervision, etc. as needed		Terry	–	50 hr	
ATA 5	**Marketing**	⊗	**Bill**	**$10,000**	**150 hr**	
ATA 5.1	Launch "Re-Made in America" campaign		Nancy	$10,000	100 hr	2-Apr
ATA 5.2	Modify website		Lynne	–	50 hr	5-May
ATA 6	**Sales**	⊗	**Harry**	–	**80 hr**	
ATA 6.1	Alert in side & outside company sales personnel		Chuck	–	40 hr	8-May
ATA 6.2	Alert sales reps and distributors		Andrew	–	40 hr	9-May
ATA 7	**Compliance**	☺	**Alice**	–	**70 hr**	
ATA 7.1	Modify compliance manual		Mike	–	50 hr	
ATA 7.2	Notify compliance agencies		Morris	–	20 hr	
ATA 8	**Information Technology**	☺	**Carl**	–	**25 hr**	
ATA 8.1	Modify ERP system as needed		Carl	–	25 hr	
ATA 9	**Accounting**	☺	**Marie**	–	**50 hr**	
ATA 9.1	Modify cost accounting sheets as needed		Joe	–	35 hr	
ATA 9.2	Modify budget and forecasts as needed		Allan	–	15 hr	
ATA 10	**Leader ship Team**	⊗	**Doris**	–	**120 hr**	
ATA 10.1	Communicate BTO & ATA to all employees		Will	–	20 hr	
ATA 10.2	Review LEAN system and modify as necessary		Molly	–	100 hr	

FIGURE 9.5

Project chart being deployed.

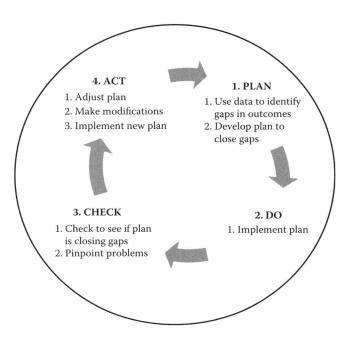

FIGURE 9.6
Deming–Shewhart continuous improvement model.

Section VI

Making the Decision to Reshore Is Just the Beginning

10

Reshoring Will Not Be a "Piece of Cake"—Many Issues to Confront and Overcome

Now that you have made the decision to reshore the USA 41 back to America, the journey has just begun. Even though the data told us reshoring was the right decision, we really will not know until we have lived with the decision for a while. After all, offshoring seemed like the right decision until we lived with the issues of manufacturing halfway around the world. Well, we are bringing it home to our own backyard and we must anticipate the problems and issues. This chapter will discuss some of the issues you might encounter when you reshore your USA 41.

SCARCITY OF SKILLED RESOURCES

The offshoring movement exported some of our most precious American resources: manufacturing jobs, manufacturing technical know-how, supply chains, role models, motivation to work in factories, and the "made in America" label. The movement was hardly perceptible at first, but as time passed, manufacturing apprentice programs dried up, the need for toolmaker jobs dwindled, and skilled machine tool operators and welders became a scarcity because of little or no demand for them. Some economists said this was a natural progression, a movement from manufacturing to technology, but for those who lost their factory jobs, it felt like their world had ended. So they learned new skills, many of lower skill levels, and found employment in many different settings, but seldom in manufacturing.

The manufacturing role models of previous generations were becoming extinct. Kids stopped tinkering in the backyard, shop, or basement, taking things apart to see how they worked and putting them back together. Sometimes the things even worked again! They did not have a lineage or inclination to learn a trade and work in the once fertile ground of American manufacturing shops. These many decades later, we find a dearth of human capital to support keeping our manufacturing onshore much less reshoring products from overseas.

Our research has shown companies that have or that are planning to reshore are doing so because of the shrinking gap in economics of offshoring and the negative circumstances of offshoring. They also want to realize the goal of having "made in America" stamped on their products again. In other words, they are pioneers of "bringing it back to America." As such, some pioneering efforts might be in order to rebuild the shrinkage of skilled resources. Since there are fewer candidates to answer ads for machine operators, welders, tool and die makers, and machinists to make your USA 41, here are two ideas that some companies are working on.

One idea to build your cadre of skilled workers is by starting an in-house apprentice program targeting the skills you will need in the future. The program can be informal and small by offering in-house training and local trade school courses to current employees. Start by identifying the education and skills required for the position and then do a gap analysis with the candidate to build a program to close the gaps. Issues such as when the candidate will receive in-house training and how outside education will be funded should be ironed out before beginning your apprentice program. An example of an apprenticeship program checklist for CNC (computer numeric control) operators is shown in Figure 10.1.

Your program does not have to focus only on the shop. You could have a program that grooms current employees for a wide variety of positions including purchasing, production control, manufacturing engineering, design engineering, accounting, supervision, and management. Such a program will not only provide a bench of candidates to fill future positions, but will allow employees to rotate through different positions throughout the company. This will increase awareness and empathy for the issues and demands of the different positions. Another benefit of having a diversified apprenticeship program is that employees will seldom get bored in one job, as they will have the skills to rotate to different positions, strengthening employee retention. Of course, as they say, every silver lining has its cloud. Employees who have learned the skills of several different positions

Apprenticeship Program
CNC Operator

_____ (name)   _____ (date begun)

	Technical Skills	Demonstrated / Achieved Sign-Off	Date
1	Write CAD Program for Simple Part		
2	Setup CNC Machine		
3	Load Tools in CNC Machine		
4	Make Adjustments for Tool Wear in CNC Machine		
5	Inspect Complex Part		
6	Perform Daily Maintenance Tasks		
7	Change Over from Part _____ to Part _____		
	Team Skills		
1	Be a Member of a Problem Solving Team		
2	Lead a Problem Solving Session		
3	Fill In for Absent Team Member		
	Education		
1	Trigonometry for Machinists		
2	Shop Etiquette		
3	Basic Machine Repair		
4	AC DC Practical Applications		
5	CAD for Machinists		
6	Practical Metallurgy		
	LEAN		
1	Toyota Production System History		
2	LEAN in America 1960s to Present		
3	LEAN for the Factory		
4	LEAN for the Office		
5	LEAN Leadership		
	Administrative Skills		
1	History of Our Company		
2	Organization Chart - Knowing Our Staff		
3	Attendance - Being Present and On Time		
4	Working with Others		
5	Filling in Shop Paperwork		
6	Filling in Quality Control Paperwork		

FIGURE 10.1
Apprenticeship program checklist.

will be very marketable in the work world and you will have to have ways to retain them.

POOR BASIC WORK SKILLS

There has been a trend with young entry-level workers lacking the basic skills to begin performing in an industrial setting. These workers might be the ones you would hire for factory or office jobs, such as janitor, clerk, laborer, or materials handler. The skills lacking in young people, cited by numerous sources, are shocking:

- Showing up for work
- Passing a drug test
- Math and computing
- Teamwork
- Attitude about work
- Workplace etiquette
- Humility
- Commitment
- Anger management

- Being on time
- Reading and retention
- Writing
- Speaking
- Conflict resolution
- Perseverance
- Flexibility
- Cooperating
- Accepting negative feedback

The reasons for the lack of these basic skills are complex and have yet to be understood fully. For example, in recent years, 50% of America's new workforce have never held basic paying jobs where they could learn these skills in low-risk settings. Summer jobs used to be the testing ground where young people could learn the art of working and earn modest wages by mowing lawns, waiting on tables, and bagging groceries at supermarkets. However, societal changes have intervened to make summer jobs scarce. Many upwardly mobile baby boomer families have the financial resources that make it unnecessary for their children to earn the extra money. Credit cards are in the hands of most teenagers, who are charging their parents' bank accounts to the ubiquitous online shopping sites and upscale malls to their hearts' content. Many kids do not need to earn the money!

Changing economic conditions have also shifted the employment direction for young people. Basic entry-level jobs are scarcer because of the movement of jobs offshored from America, mostly manufacturing jobs.

When manufacturing leaves, so do some or all of the jobs needed to support manufacturers, such as:

- *Raw materials* made by:
  - Steel mills
  - Casting foundries
  - Forging shops
  - Sheet metal levelers and sizers
  - Stamping shops
  - Polymer manufacturers
  - Fastener manufacturers
  - Welding supply companies

- *Machines* made by:
  - Metal-forming machine companies
  - Metal-bending machine companies
  - Metal-burning machine companies
  - Laser machine companies
  - Stamping machine companies
  - CNC machine companies
  - Conventional machine tool companies
  - Coordinate measuring machine companies
  - Inspection hand-device companies
  - Welding machine companies
  - Hand-tool companies
  - Cutting-tool companies
  - Plastics-forming companies
  - Injection-molding machine companies
  - Conveyor companies
  - Three-dimensional printer companies

- *Services* provided by:
  - Trucking companies
  - Uniform cleaning companies
  - Carpet cleaning companies
  - Market research firms
  - Website development firms
  - Copy shops
  - Fastener suppliers

- Janitorial services
- Machine repair services

Think of the thousands of entry-level jobs that are now scarce, where young people do not have the opportunity to:

- Learn how to go to work every day and arrive on time
- Work with others and learn to deal with their differences
- Have the feeling of accomplishment when objectives are met
- Experience disappointment when objectives are not met
- Discover why objectives were not met and what to do next time

The domino effect of these companies (manufacturers and their suppliers) either going out of business or reducing their workforce is only the beginning for making jobs for young people difficult to find. Consider the numerous local businesses that had sprung up over time providing services to the employees of those companies, for example:

- Barber and beauty shops
- Florists
- Restaurants
- Bakeries
- General merchandise shops
- Tire stores
- Hardware stores
- Dentists
- Car repair shops
- Pet stores
- Bar and grills
- Auto repair shops
- Auto supply shops
- Bicycle shops
- Grocery stores
- GP physicians

Additionally, young people are lacking in developing fundamental job skills because of the pressure put on them by society, their parents, their contemporaries, and themselves, by preparing for scarce professional positions. They are devoting their summers and free time to bone up for the increasingly difficult entrance exams into name-brand undergraduate and graduate schools.

This is an interesting place we find ourselves, a Catch-22. Young people seem to lose any way they move. We, the members of American society, have a responsibility to rise above the current situation to rebuild basic job skills in our youth and others who still have not yet developed them.

If you are a *young person* lacking entry-level job skills, we encourage you to take the initiative to find situations where you can experience the work environment by:

- Considering any job, even if it feels beneath your status
- Not waiting for jobs to come to you, but going out and finding them
- Networking with friends to find the job right for you; they may already have a list of jobs they have passed over
- Using the Internet to find jobs where you live or are attending school:
  - *Craigslist* has postings for over 40 job categories, from accounting to writing. Craigslist also has a place for you to post your resumé or simply describe your skills and desire to do work for specific types of jobs.
  - *CareerBuilder* allows you to searches for jobs by area code and type. You can also search by entering keywords (e.g. "part time", "entry level", etc.).
- Not getting discouraged if you do not find a job right away and keeping on looking
- Putting your best foot forward when you call on a prospective employer by being well dressed, well groomed, and well spoken
- Rehearsing your personal introduction with a friend before you meet your prospective employer
- If you still cannot find the job for you, inventing your own part-time business that will allow you to get the experience of working with others and customers (Some ideas for part-time jobs are home pet watching, dog walking, house cleaning, house painting, lawn mowing, and car detailing.)

If you are a *parent* of a young person lacking entry-level job skills, we encourage you to persuade him or her to find a part-time job during the school year or a full-time job in the summer. Use the preceding list to help the young person identify and be prepared for this first job. Set the stage for his or her not only wanting a job, but also needing it by paring back on allowances and amenities. Give your children reasons for having a job (e.g., their paying for part of their education, paying their fair share for gas in the family car, and setting up a savings account of their own with goals they can achieve and maintain). Parents, this writer included, have had a desire of wanting our children to have it better than we did growing up. However, as we gave them more, they lost some of the experiences and values that could have prepared them for the work world. Simply said, the more our children have, the less need they have for a job!

As parents, we can also put less pressure on our children by not insisting they climb the ladder sooner than they are prepared to do so. We can help them by developing a "job diary" with them that will facilitate their discovering the important elements of their early jobs career, for example:

- How to relate to their supervisor
- Getting along with co-workers
- Getting to work on time every day
- Dealing with an imperfect work environment
- Having the "thrill of victory and the agony of defeat"
- Learning from their mistakes
- Earning and saving money
- Preparing for their next job

An example of a jobs diary can be found in Figure 10.2. It is a radar screen of the things a young person should be aware of in a new job. The essential part about the jobs diary is that you and your son or daughter develop it together, and then you coach him or her along the way, giving advice and feedback. This personalizes your role in developing young people to become the next generation of American workers in factories and offices.

If you are a *business owner* or a *person of influence* working in a company, you might think about setting up an introductory training session with all your new employees, briefing them on the basic job skills you expect them to have or develop. A pocket or wallet size card listing skills and expectations could be something they carry with them or in their wallet or purse. (See Figure 10.3.) This might already be part of your code of conduct.

If you are truly a progressive company and believe that employee behavior and development is your responsibility, you might want to pair a new employee with a mentor who can guide the new employee in the journey with your company. The job diary can be used with the employee expectations to provide a focus for the new employee during the first few weeks with you.

In summary, if we are serious about resurrecting our workforce, each of us must take responsibility and devise our own way of contributing. We have provided some ideas and models for young people, parents, and business owners and influential businesspeople. However, the list could go on to include people in chambers of commerce, business development departments, professional societies, trade schools, etc. Hopefully, some

Job Diary

_____ (job description) _____ (company)
_____ (beginning salary) _____ (ending salary)
_____ (hours worked) _____ (days worked)
_____ (boss's name) _____ (start date - end date)
_____ (co-worker name) _____ (co-worker name)

	My Boss	Notes	Date
1	Describe as stern or kind or ……		
2	Sets clear expectations?		
3	Explains job in easy to understand words?		
4	Praises when I/we do a good job?		
5	Explains what happened when I/we did a poor job?		
6	Does not constantly look over my/our shoulder?		
7	Sets a good example for us?		
8	Someone easy to talk to?		
9	Someone I admire?		
10	What I would do differently?		
	My Co-Workers		
1	Meeting new people		
2	Learning how people are different from me		
3	Dealing with their differences		
4	Sharing my background		
5	Asking about their background		
6	Learning how to compromise		
7	Having a negative experience		
8	Learning from the negative experience		
9	Having a good experience		
10	How to have more good experiences		
	The Job		
1	Arriving on time		
2	Rules and regulations		
3	Learning to do the job		
4	Making mistakes		
5	Learning why I made my mistakes		
6	Doing the job differently next time		
7	Having the right tools to do my job		
8	Dealing with not having the right tools		
9	Having a good experience		
10	How to have more good experiences		
	When the Job Ended		
1	Learning about being an effective boss		
2	Learning about co-workers		
3	Learning about the company		
4	How I said goodbye		
5	What my boss said to me		
6	What my co-workers said to me		
7	How much money I made & saved		
8	What kind of job I want next		
9	What kind of job I am prepared for next		
10	What I need to do for my next job		

FIGURE 10.2
Job diary.

Welcome to our Company

As members of our company there are certain things that we expect of each other regardless of position or title

1. Be at your work station or desk ready to work on time each day.
2. Be honest with each other—do not lie, steal, or cheat.
3. Be respectful of your co-workers' rights and differences.
4. Have a positive attitude about your job.
5. Don't give up when your job seems difficult.
6. Try to resolve conflicts you have with your co-workers or supervisors.
7. Be flexible in your job, you might be asked to work at another position.
8. Learn new skills either on your own or through company programs.
9. Work as a team when asked or when you see the need—help each other.
10. Give feedback in constructive ways to your co-workers and superiors.

FIGURE 10.3
Employee expectations.

ideas that have been presented will get us started to develop the work ethic, build basic work skills in our young people, and set them on their way to contribute to reshoring manufacturing jobs back to America.

ANEMIC SUPPLY CHAINS

Also damaged by offshoring is the weakening of supply chains in America. This is especially true for products that are dominated by Chinese manufacturing, such as cell phones, bicycles, and cloth goods. In fact, many product components cannot be found made in America at all. As you begin your search for suppliers, you might discover it challenging to find them, especially in your geographic area. Your best suppliers could be thousands of miles away, with mediocre suppliers just down the street. The challenge is to find the supplier that best meets the needs of your USA 41 and your business. Even in the finest companies, departmental viewpoints of who is the best supplier have different meanings. The following are extreme examples of how the various departments might choose the "best" supplier for the reshored USA 41:

- Purchasing:
  - Lowest unit price

- Lowest transportation costs
- Best payment terms

- Engineering:
  - Best physical properties
  - Best to meet final engineering specifications

- Manufacturing:
  - Easiest to set up
  - Easiest to machine
  - Easiest to assemble

- Plant facilities:
  - Smallest inventory
  - Easiest to unload from delivery truck

- Marketing:
  - Will appeal to customers
  - Will develop brand loyalty

- Customer Service:
  - Easiest for customers to use
  - Will not break down
  - Will not cause customer complaints
  - Low warranty risk

With the current supply chain situation, it might be difficult to find suppliers close by (where you can control quality and production) who can meet all the departments' needs of your USA 41 in its current design. In the previous chapters, we told the story of General Electric reshoring its water heaters and redesigning them to meet many departmental needs.

Our inclusive 360° method for making decisions threads its way to the redesign, too. Assembling your department experts and managers will provide the best redesign by asking them to evaluate several redesign options, and the sourced materials, against criteria that will satisfy your collective needs. We have developed a design comparison chart, shown in Figure 10.4, for evaluating two redesigns and the sourced materials for the USA 41. The product design criteria we have chosen for comparison include:

Comparison Chart

Product Design #1						
Purchased Parts		Design for:				
Forging	Special Bearing	Function	Supply	Mfg	Assy	
Total Score						**192**

Product Design #1						
Purchased Parts		Design for:				
Forging	Special Bearing	Function	Supply	Mfg	Assy	
Total Score						**113**

Design Criteria

Function

Easy to Use	Does the Job!	Right Weight	Looks Good	Price	Total Score
Design #1					
8	9	5	4	2	28
Design #2					
5	4	4	6	3	22

28

22

Supply

Avail-able	Lead Time	Distfm Plant	Terms	Cost	Total Score %
Design #1 - Forging					
8	5	10	9	7	39
Design #1 - Special Bearing					
7	7	8	8	10	40
Design #2 - Forging					
5	4	5	4	3	21
Design #2 - Special Bearing					
3	5	6	4	3	21

39

40

21

21

Manufacture

Easy to Set-Up	Simple Design	Cuts Easy	Clean-Up	Mfg Time	Total Score %
Design #1					
8	7	9	8	10	42
Design #2					
5	3	9	4	6	27

42

27

Assembly

Parts Fit	Hand Tools	Power Tools	Slip Factor	Assy Time	Total Score %
Design #1					
8	9	8	10	8	43
Design #2					
4	6	7	2	3	22

43

22

FIGURE 10.4
Product redesign comparison.

- Function:
  1. Easy to use: customers can operate the USA 41 with minimal instructions.
  2. Does the job: it outperforms the competition.
  3. Right weight: it is not too light, not too heavy…feels just right.
  4. Looks good: customer is proud to show it off.
  5. Price: the USA 41s "fly off the shelves" because of their best value.
- Supply:
  1. Available: components, assemblies, and subassemblies are available.
  2. Lead time: delivery from supplier is quick after order is placed.
  3. Distance: supplier is less than 1 hour away.
  4. Terms: payment terms are favorable to cash conversion cycle.

     5. Cost: cost is low to support high sales margins.
- Manufacture:
  1. Setup: it is easy to set up in machine tools.
  2. Simple design: the manufacturing process is uncomplicated.
  3. Cuts easily: material is easy to remove and near net shape.
  4. Cleanup: it is easy to clean up machines and work areas.
  5. Time: short manufacturing times support high margins.
- Assembly:
  1. Parts fit: there is no need to mess with making parts fit.
  2. Hand tools: no complicated hand tools are required.
  3. Power tools: no complicated power tools are required.
  4. Slip factor: parts are made to correct tolerance for slip-fit assembly.
  5. Time: short assembly times support high margins.

Our comparison chart is for high-level demonstration purposes only. Elements we ask you to add include:

- Weighting of the descriptors under each heading, for example:
  - *Easy to use* might be more important than *has the right weight* under **Function.**
  - *Terms* might be less important than *lead time* under **Supply.**
  - *Cleanup* might be less important than *cuts easily* under **Manufacture.**
  - *Time* might be more important than *hand tools* under **Assembly.**

- Method for understanding the design options, for example:
  - Discussion of the product designs led by Marketing and Engineering
  - Discussion of the purchased parts led by Purchasing
  - Discussion of the manufacture and assembly led by Manufacturing, including shop workers
  - Discussion of the functionality led by Customer Service
  - Discussion of material movement led by Plant Facilities

- Method for reaching design change options, for example:
  - Members from each department asking questions, making comments, making suggestions
  - Brainstorming changes, substitutions, deletions
  - Making design changes based on consensus
  - Reevaluating the design changes to the top two choices

- Scoring the top two as demonstrated on the design comparison chart
- Choosing the design with the higher score *and* consensus by all department members

This method is only a suggestion, but the concept of involvement in making the best redesign decision of the USA 41 will yield the best result to satisfy all departments' needs, with the customers' interests first and foremost.

LOCATION

Where to reshore your USA 41 is another consideration. Our bias is to have your production as close to your operation as possible to avoid the hassles of remote manufacturing previously discussed. Five hundred miles is better than halfway around the world, but it is impossible to run down to the manufacturing floor to see how production is going if you need to or want just to check out a few things or talk to the operators to see how everything is going. However, this book is about helping you make choices, and with that, the following are two considerations about where to set up your reshoring operations.

Incentives

States, counties, and cities are competing with each other to offer incentives for companies to set up manufacturing operations in their areas. The reason for the incentives is obvious: to bring in more jobs to increase tax revenue and stimulate their economies. The multiplier effect that manufacturing has on the economy has been documented many times. The National Association of Manufacturers states that, in 2012, "…for every dollar spent on manufacturing, another $1.48[1] is added to the economy, the highest multiplier effect of any other sector." Searching for incentives may or may not make sense for you. It depends on many factors, such as if you are already considering moving operations, your proximity to an entity offering incentives, etc. For example, a caster manufacturer in Hamilton, Ohio, made a strategic decision to increase its manufacturing capacity and had two options. Option one was to build an additional building on the current site, which is a 100-year-old facility. Option two was to construct a new, green field facility. Hamilton, Ohio, is close to the Indiana boarder, so the company explored incentives in Indiana as well as incentives within Hamilton to build the new facility. They were delighted to find that both the city of Hamilton and Dearborn County, Indiana, offered incentives. At the time of this writing, the company had not made the decision of whether to construct a new facility or build on the current site, but it had more options than expected—and all for the asking.

The spectrum of incentives is broad, deep, and varying. Just by exploring the Internet by inserting "(state name) incentives for manufacturers," results are readily available. To demonstrate, when the phrase "Alabama…" is inserted, these are a sampling of its offerings:

- Income taxes
  - Full deduction for all federal income taxes apportioned to Alabama, creating a significantly reduced net effective rate
  - Net operating losses carried forward 15 years
- Property taxes
  - Inventories and goods in process not taxed
  - Pollution control equipment statutorily exempt from property taxation
  - Exemption of all tangible personal property being warehoused in Alabama for shipment to a destination outside the state
  - Abatements by cities, counties, and public authorities to qualifying projects may include noneducational state, county, and city property taxes for a period of up to 10 years
- Sales and use taxes
  - Raw materials used by manufacturers or compounders specifically exempt from sales and use taxation
  - Pollution control equipment statutorily exempt from taxation
  - Credit for sales and use tax paid to another state and its subdivisions
  - Exemption for quality control testing and donations to charitable entities

As can be seen from the Alabama example, the offerings and terms are quite detailed. How they fit your needs will be determined by other factors, such as:

- Whether current employees would be disadvantaged by a move
- Movement of shop and office equipment and machinery disruption
- How a move fits with your long-term strategy
- The effect a move would have on your current supply chain

- The cost of relocating versus remaining at your current facility
- The many other factors that only you can determine

We are not endorsing Alabama, Indiana, Ohio, or any other state's interest in bringing manufacturing to their states. However, we are suggesting that your circumstances might be such that exploring incentives, even in your own state, county, or city, might make reshoring your USA 41 even more attractive.

Right-to-Work States

Whether you are for or against organized labor, you should know about the "right-to-work" laws so that you can decide how it might affect your decision where to reshore your USA 41.

Right to work had its beginnings in 1947, immediately following WWII, with enactment of the Labor Management Relations Act, also known as the Taft–Hartley Act. During WWII, organized labor agreed to limit strikes and work with management to produce war materiel to win the war. However, Republicans were concerned that when the war ended, unions would renew labor campaigns to increase wages and benefits that were constrained during the war. Such actions, they felt, would militate against reconstruction in the United States and America's planned actions to help the rest of the world in post-WWII reconstruction.

The Taft–Hartley Act essentially added a list of *unfair labor practices by unions* to the list of *unfair labor practices by employers* to the National Labor Relations Act (NLRA), which was signed into law by President Roosevelt and enacted in 1935. In other words, it leveled the playing field between employers and labor. The NLRA guarantees employees the right to form trade unions, engage in collective bargaining, and strike if necessary. A key element of the Taft–Hartley Act allows individual states to pass right-to-work laws that ban closed union shops. A closed shop is one in which employees must join the union as a condition of employment. An open shop is one in which the employee is not required to belong to the union or pay union dues in order to work for an employer. That means that an employee could choose to stay with the union and pay union dues or leave it by free choice and not pay dues. Since right-to-work states and non-right-to-work states exist, it is worth your while to study the situation. As of this writing, 24 states have passed right-to-work legislation.

There is much debate concerning the degree to which right-to-work states are good for all employees, employers, unions, our country, and the global economy. Pro-right-to-work advocates cite employers having more freedom in making business decisions due to the diluted monopoly of unions. Unions say employees who do not want to join their union reap the benefits of collective bargaining without paying union dues. These are valid opinions but are more qualitative versus quantitative. Even the quantitative data are not clear.

One right-to-work advocate[2] contrasted five economic factors based on analyses from the Bureau of Labor Statistics, US Census Bureau, US Patent and Research Office, and Bureau of Economic Analysis showing the benefits of right-to-work states:

1. Percentage growth in non-farm private sector employees (1995–2005)
   a. Right-to-work states: 12.9%
   b. Non-right-to-work states: 6.0%
2. Average poverty rate, adjusted for cost of living (2002–2004)
   a. Right-to-work states: 8.5%
   b. Non-right-to-work states: 10.1%
3. Percentage growth in patents annually granted (1995–2005)
   a. Right-to-work states: 33.0%
   b. Non-right-to-work states: 11.0%
4. Percentage growth in real personal income (1995–2005)
   a. Right-to-work states: 26.0%
   b. Non-right-to-work states: 19.0%
5. Percentage growth in number of people covered by employment-based private health insurance (1995–2005):
   a. Right-to-work states: 8.5%
   b. Non-right-to-work states: 0.7%

On the other hand, a non-right-to-work advocate[3] says the following about right-to-work states:

- Working families in states with right-to-work laws earn lower wages.
  - On average, workers in states with right-to-work laws earn $5,538 a year less than workers in states without these laws.
- Right-to-work states spend less on education.
  - Right-to-work states spend $2,671 less per pupil on elementary and secondary education than free-bargaining states do.

- Right-to-work states have higher workplace fatality rates.
  - According to data from the Bureau of Labor Statistics, the rate of workplace deaths is 52.9% higher in states with right-to-work laws.
- Right-to-work laws do not improve living standards; unions improve living standards.
  - Overall, union members earn 28% ($198) more per week than non-union workers. Hispanic union members earn 50% ($258) more each week than nonunion Hispanics, and African Americans earn 29% ($168) more each week if they are union members.
  - Of private sector union workers, 78% have access to medical insurance through their jobs, compared with 51% of nonunion workers. And 77% of private sector union workers have access to a guaranteed (defined benefit) retirement plan through their jobs, compared with just 20% of nonunion workers.
  - Only 2.9% of union workers are uninsured, compared with 14.2% of nonunion workers.

As one can see, who is telling the story slants the facts to the teller's advantage. Again, our advice is to be aware that right-to-work states exist and determine if that will influence your reshoring decision.

INCREASING OPERATIONAL EFFECTIVENESS WITH LEAN

Even though Lean has proven to be the way to produce products at the lowest overall cost with the highest quality and best customer satisfaction, very few American manufacturers have implemented a full-blown, completely developed Lean management system at their company. By "full-blown, completely developed" we mean the entire company has adopted and adapted to the principles of Lean. On the other hand, many companies have dabbled in Lean—meaning they have tried some of the more popular and easy to implement Lean elements (e.g., 5S, shop kaizen, setup reduction, and kanban). More than half of those have abandoned any systematic approach of going further or even maintaining what they have done. It is no wonder employees look at management as just waiting for the next "program of the month" to come along, but it is not management's fault; they are simply victims of human behavior.

We humans act on scenarios in which we believe the consequences will be *immediate* and *certain,* whether the results are positive or negative. Consequences believed to come to fruition in the *future* or that are *uncertain* have less chance of being acted upon. If you do not believe this, let us look at just a few examples:

First Two Scenarios: **Consequences Are Immediate and Certain**

1. "That cheeseburger on the menu looks delicious, and I'm starving."
   - The consequence:
     - **Positive:** "I haven't had a cheeseburger in weeks, oh boy."
     - **Immediate:** "We can have that cheeseburger right away for you, Sir."
     - **Certain:** "We have the best cheeseburgers in town here, Sir!"
   - The action:
     - "I'll have the cheeseburger, Miss, and with fries and a milk shake, please."
2. "I just had a consultation with my doctor. I have three spots on my lungs that showed up on my x-ray and my biopsy came back positive. I have the beginnings of lung cancer."
   - The consequence:
     - **Negative:** "Sir, yes, you do have cancer and it can spread to your lymph nodes."
     - **Immediate:** "You need to begin chemotherapy tomorrow and stop smoking now."
     - **Certain:** "If you don't do as prescribed, you have 3 weeks to live!"
   - The action:
     - "I'll sign up for the chemo right now and please throw these cigarettes away for me, Doctor."

Next Two Scenarios: **Consequences Are Future and Uncertain**

1. "If I begin investing every week starting now, when I am 25 years old, I will have lots of money for retirement when I am 65."
   - The consequence:
     - **Positive:** "I'll have a great retirement nest egg."
     - **Future:** "I won't be 65 for another 40 years. That's a long time from now."
     - **Uncertain:** "Heck, I might die tomorrow, and I want that new convertible."
   - The action:
     - "I'll get around to getting a savings account someday."

2. "If I don't quit smoking cigarettes, I will get lung cancer."
   - The consequence:
     - **Negative:** "I'll die a horrible death."
     - **Future:** "But, I feel OK today."
     - **Uncertain:** "My father is 90 years old and still smokes."
   - The action:
     - "I'll get around to quitting someday. Gee, I need to stop at the store for more cigarettes."

These scenarios help explain why most long-term Lean programs are abandoned. After the novelty and quick hits from 5S and kaizen events wear off, the effort needed for sustainment is long term with less than certain results. Changes in management can also explain redirecting resources from Lean to other scenarios that are more immediate and certain, such as fighting fires. Whether we want to admit it or not we have a love–hate relationship with firefighting. We hate them because they consume resources and redirect us from our "real jobs," but we love fighting fires because of the "feel-goods" we get in putting the flames out and saying, "I fixed that one."

Unfortunately, implementing a long-term Lean program is neither immediate nor certain. That is why we previously described how to develop your hoshin plan to reshore. By its design, hoshin planning has you look toward future desired results (future—uncertain—consequences) and break them down into actions you can take now that will show more immediate results (immediate—certain—consequences). Hoshin supports the Biblical quote, "The spirit is willing, but the flesh is weak," by having us identify short-term targets on which we can focus resources that will give us the feel-goods we need to proceed further. Equipped with hoshin planning to achieve long-term goals, you have a greater certainty of implementing your own "full-blown, completely developed" Lean management system by adopting and adapting to the principles of Lean.

The principles of Lean are really quite simple:

1. Keep the value steam moving at maximum velocity.
2. Eliminate waste that stops, slows down, or diverts the value stream (Figure 10.5).
3. Concentrate first on removing waste rather than speeding up the value-adding operations in the value stream.

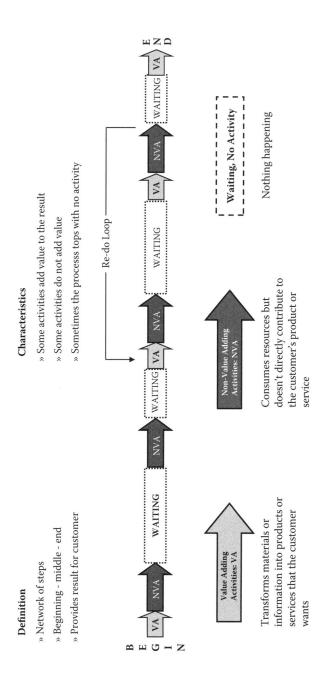

FIGURE 10.5
The value stream.

1. Conduct P-Q Analysis of Value Stream Set – Pareto Analysis
2. Conduct Value Stream Analysis – Spaghetti Chart
3. Conduct Process Route Analysis
4. Develop Product Families
5. Collect Base Line Data
6. Rationalize Process – Kaikaku
7. Conduct 5S Program
8. Reduce Process Waste – Kaizen
9. Collect Processing Data
10. Develop Average Weighted Capacity Analysis – Takt Time
11. Lay Out Product Family Cell
12. Develop Standard Work for Doers & Leaders
13. Rationalize Change Overs – SMED
14. Improve quality – Jidoka & Poka-Yoke
15. Smooth Production – Heijunka
16. Institute Material Control – Kan Ban
17. Develop & Institute Cell Controls – QCDS
18. Create Focus Product Teams – SDWT
19. Improve Equipment Availability – TOM
20. Develop Visual Management – Andon

FIGURE 10.6
Lean tools for the shop.

4. Engage everyone to look for and remove waste called the evil-*ings:*

Batch*ing*	Scrapp*ing*	Watch*ing*	Miss*ing* info
Sort*ing*	Walk*ing*	Search*ing*	Miss*ing* parts
Stopp*ing*	Mov*ing*	Approv*ing*	Wait*ing*
Rework*ing*	Unnecessary process*ing*		

5. Develop standard work and metrics for performance in each value stream.
6. Reduce defects and variation in each step of the value stream.
7. Make continuous improvement a way of policy.

Adopting the principles of Lean is more difficult. It means using the Lean tools throughout your business (office—shop—suppliers) to achieve the results of Lean in each value stream. Figure 10.6 is a listing of the Lean

1. Define Major Value Stream Processes
2. Prioritize via Pre-Established Criteria
3. Select Resource Support Team
   1. Process Owners
4. Select Process Improvement Team
5. Conduct Office Kaizen
   1. Rationalize Process - Reduce Process Waste
6. Develop & Institute Cell Controls – QCDS
7. Create Focus Product Teams – SDWT
8 Develop Standard Work for Doers & Leaders
9. Develop Visual Management – Andon

FIGURE 10.7
Lean tools for the office.

tools in the order they might be used on a typical value stream setting in the *shop.*

Listed in Figure 10.7 are the Lean tools in the order they might be used on a typical value stream setting in the *office.*

From our experience in helping organizations learn these tools, it takes about five iterations of each setting, shop and office, to become proficient in them. However, learning the Lean tools is just the beginning. Sustaining the Lean effort is the challenge and therefore the reason for applying hoshin planning. Our experience has also shown the need for the leaders of the organization to be engaged thoroughly in the Lean implementation, as they and the entire company learn to use the Lean tools. The organization-wide Lean infrastructure (Figure 10.8) will ensure the active engagement of the leadership team.

This is how the organization-wide Lean infrastructure works:

- The leadership team
  - Drives all Lean activities
    - They have hands-on involvement.
    - They prioritize the value streams (Figure 10.5), for applying the Lean tools for the shop (Figure 10.6) and office (Figure 10.7).

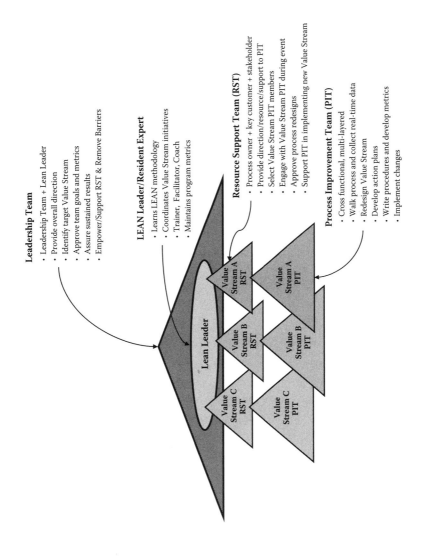

Leadership Team
- Leadership Team + Lean Leader
- Provide overall direction
- Identify target Value Stream
- Approve team goals and metrics
- Assure sustained results
- Empower/Support RST & Remove Barriers

LEAN Leader/Resident Expert
- Learns LEAN methodology
- Coordinates Value Stream initiatives
- Trainer, Facilitator, Coach
- Maintains program metrics

Resource Support Team (RST)
- Process owner + key customer + stakeholder
- Provide direction/resource/support to PIT
- Select Value Stream PIT members
- Engage with Value Stream PIT during event
- Approve process redesigns
- Support PIT in implementing new Value Stream

Process Improvement Team (PIT)
- Cross functional, multi-layered
- Walk process and collect real-time data
- Redesign Value Stream
- Develop action plans
- Write procedures and develop metrics
- Implement changes

FFIGURE 10.8
Organization-wide Lean infrastructure.

- They assign one member of the leadership team to lead a resource support team (RST), which will lead the value stream activity assigned by the leadership team.
- The RST
  - Is composed of
    - The members of the leadership team assigned to lead the value stream activity
    - Other members:
      - The process owner
      - A customer of the value stream
      - A key stakeholder of the value stream
  - Identifies the process improvement team (PIT) members, who will be the ones applying the Lean tools for shop or Lean tools for office to the assigned value stream
  - Provides resources and support for the PIT to carry out the implementation assigned by the leadership team
- The PIT
  - Is composed of
    - One of the RST members agreed to by the leadership team
    - Five to seven persons who
      - Are involved with the value stream on a daily basis
      - Know the value stream inside and out
      - Are interested in seeing the value stream improved
      - Are not afraid to speak their minds about the value stream
      - Have the time to apply the Lean tools to the value stream
      - Note: At least one member of the PIT should be a person outside the value stream so he or she can ask the dumb question, "Why do you do it that way?"
- The Lean leader
  - Is a person who has the skills to train, facilitate, and coach the following in all aspects of Lean:
    - Leadership team
    - Resource support team
    - Process improvement team
  - Is skilled at interacting with all levels of people and has organization development skills as well as technical know-how of the shop and office
  - Keeps all training materials, documents, and results of all value stream activities

The organization-wide Lean infrastructure is very effective by keeping everyone focused and engaged on the Lean implementation. Adapting the principles of Lean to your organization is the secret to long-term sustainment (i.e., to inculcate the philosophy, tools, models, and metrics into your organization's culture by creating your own Lean management system).

CREATING YOUR OWN LEAN MANAGEMENT SYSTEM

The previous section encouraged you to adopt the tools of Lean in order to manufacture your USA 41 competitively at the lowest cost possible and with the highest quality. This section will give you some thoughts to create your own Lean management system as many other successful companies have done to supercharge their organizational effectiveness.

Toyota is the foundation of all Lean management systems. Although their system is commonly known as the Toyota *production* system (TPS), it is actually the Toyota *management* system and it defines how each department operates and how each employee, from company president to water spider (material handler) on the floor, should conduct himself or herself. The Toyota production system is composed of these principles:

- Continuous improvement
  - Kaizen every process throughout the company including suppliers, shop, and office.
  - Solve recurring problems by determining the root cause—ask "Why?" five times.
- Building processes that add value
  - Standardize work: write standard work for every work task.
  - Pull production: produce only what has been ordered by the customer.
  - Build quality into the process: make the process such that it is impossible to make defects.
  - Allow anyone to stop a process that is making defects.
- Respect for people
  - Teach employees to be experts in their jobs and in continuous improvement activities.

- Make every effort so each employee is performing only work that adds value to the customer.
  - Foster teamwork in every department.
- Long-term thinking
  - Make decisions and actions based on today but plan and act for the future.
  - Stay the course, even at the expense of short-term goals.
- Managing upstream processes
  - Work with suppliers and *their* suppliers to provide defect-free materials.
  - Facilitate just-in-time delivery of materials.

The details of the Toyota production system seem endless, written in numerous books, websites, and, surprisingly, Toyota's own website. We encourage you to go there (http://www.toyota-global.com/) and read for yourself under these headings:

- Toyota Production System
- Guiding Principles at Toyota
- Five Main Principles of (Mr.) Toyoda, the founder of Toyota
- Toyota's Corporate Social Responsibility Policy
- Toyota's Global Vision
- Globalizing and Localizing Manufacturing
- Toyota Code of Conduct

The Toyota production system is a work in progress that had its genesis in post-World War II Japanese reconstruction; it is a system that is over a half century in the making. Our suggestion is that you consider developing your own Lean management system. If you already have a management system, you might find some of the discussion helpful to improve your own system. First, a caveat: creating a management system, much less a Lean management system, will require:

- Benchmarking
- Education
- Creativity
- Inspiration
- Resources
- Time

- Money
- Patience
- Perseverance
- A system to stay focused and, most importantly,
- Leadership

If you can agree to dealing with these issues, then proceed. If not, you might want to do more research and wait until you are ready.

A good place to start thinking about designing your Lean management system is to define the breadth and depth you want it to apply. Breadth is the horizontal expanse of the system's application. A 100% wide expanse will affect every department in the organization and the organization's suppliers:

- Departments
  - Executive
    - Leadership team
    - Managers
    - Supervisors
  - Finance and Accounting
  - Marketing
  - Research and Development
  - Engineering
  - Purchasing
  - Manufacturing
  - Quality Assurance
  - Customer Support
- Suppliers
  - Manufacturing materials
  - Physical services
  - Consulting services

Depth is the degree to which the system will govern the activities of each department. A 100% depth of governance will affect every element of how work is done in each department. If the governance is too detailed, it will be difficult to do business (like putting on handcuffs). We have seen some management systems that are so detailed that any slight variation from the system is a nonconformance requiring an explanation for the deviation, a root cause analysis, and a corrective action plan. It might be wise to find middle ground and avoid either extreme of too detailed versus not detailed enough.

An example of middle ground is traffic signs. Black-and-white speed limit signs tell us how fast we are permitted by law to go, yellow-and-black speed limit signs are suggestions of managing our speed to navigate around turns and hazards. Stop signs tell us we must stop at intersections; yield signs tell us where to be considerate of pedestrians and other vehicles.

It is a matter of using common sense in determining the depth your system will govern the departments within your organization. We suggest you begin by listing your departments and then determine the extent to which you want the system to provide governance over each in specific categories, such as standard work, metrics, and frequency of kaizens (Figure 10.9). Note that the examples are based on our experience with organizations just beginning their journey in developing a Lean management system.

Exploring each category of governance we will begin with "standard work"—written instructions that describe how work is to be performed on a specific task. Depending upon the task and the criticality of the task, the details of the standard work will vary. A rule of thumb in determining the level of detail needed for standard work is to consider:

- The rigor required to perform the job correctly
- The variation that can be tolerated
- The criticality of the outcome

Our experience is that the closer one gets to actual manufacturing and the processes that support it, the higher the details for standard work need to be. Machine operators, assemblers, welders, painters, and other shop personnel that do repetitive jobs require very detailed standard work so that engineering design specifications are met for the product. On the other hand, customer support personnel, who handle a variety of issues when customers call in with complaints or questions, require more flexibility in doing their jobs.

Although certain aspects of the standard work for customer support should be detailed (e.g., how the call is taken, the greeting, the questions asked, the disposition routine for returning goods, answering commonly asked questions, and passing the call to a higher authority), there must be space for good judgment. This is the time for a "corral" approach, or defining the boundaries within which customer support may work independently and where they must involve others.

In addition to how the job is performed, standard work also defines the quality requirements and time expectations to complete the job. Using the

Lean Management System - Departmental Governance									
Department (listed below)	**Standard Work** System Governance			**Metrics** System Governance			**Feq of Kaizens** System Governance		
	Hi	Med	Low	Hi	Med	Low	Hi	Med	Low
Key Personnel									
Board of Directors			L			L			L
President			L		M				L
Vice Presidents			L		M				L
Directors			L		M				L
Managers		M			M				L
Supervisors	H			H			H		
Employees	H			H			H		
HR									
Hiring Process		M		H					L
Training & Dev'l		M		H					L
Marketing									
Product Dev'l		M			M				L
Advertising		M			M				L
Sales									
Outside sales		M		H				M	
Inside sales		M		H				M	
Engineering									
Design engineering	H			H				M	
Mfg. engineering	H			H				M	
Customer Support									
Warranty claims		M		H				M	
Customer service		M		H				M	
Operations									
Purchasing		M		H				M	
Production control		M		H				M	
Manufacturing	H			H			H		
Shipping & receiving	H			H				M	
Quality Assurance									
Quality planning	H					M		M	
Quality control	H					M		M	
Process control	H					M		M	
Inspection	H			H				M	
Finance									
Cost accounting	H			H			H		
Billing	H			H			H		

FIGURE 10.9

Lean management system—departmental governance.

preceding examples, the workers in the shop are manufacturing products repetitively to a planned time and have rigid engineering specifications. Their standard work will be very detailed, defining the product's dimensional and characteristic features and the time allotted to make each part. The customer support person will have less defined time expectations because each call will be different, requiring varying times to take care of the customer. The quality expectations will also be less exacting; however, some definition of the outcome of the call will be defined (e.g., the satisfaction of the customer at the end of the call, the resolution of a problem, etc.). The board of directors, president, and directors fall into the category of having less defined standard work. Their workdays are filled with uncertainty and they need the flexibility to work through the myriad issues that befall them.

It will be necessary eventually to write the standard work for each department, by job, as defined by your system. As one can imagine, this is a task that will require prioritization, planning, a process for defining the standard work, involvement by the process owners, and project management to ensure that standard work is written and followed. Suggestions for how to go about this will be discussed later. Let us now go to the metrics.

Metrics are customized charts associated with the standard work and maintained by the person doing the work. The metrics document the outcome of the work and any variations, trends, and other characteristics of the task. In a Lean system, the key metrics are quality, cost, and delivery and, when in the shop, safety is added. The metrics are kept visible for all to see, which is common in a Lean system—the concept of visual management. The principle is the ability to see how each department is performing its task toward the overall objectives of the organization as shown in Figure 10.10.

When determining the breadth and depth of how each department measures its outcomes, it is prudent to follow the Pareto principle, which states that 80% of the effects come from 20% of the causes. However, on occasion, there may be a specific process that you might want to chart because you want to target your efforts to improve its outcomes. The process improvement tool used in Lean is kaizen.

Kaizen (translated as "change for the better") is a team-based approach of improving processes by using the scientific method of:

1. Studying the current process
2. Developing a hypothesis for what "better" could look like if specific changes are made

Department	Task	Goal	Chart
President	Send newsletter to all employees	Send newsletter monthly	Newsletters sent by date by month
Human Resources	Hire shop employees	Five new shop employees hired by May 5	Number of shop employees hired by month versus feedback from shop on quality of new employee
Marketing	Introduce new products	Introduce new products A and B June 20	Progress chart of introduction by month
Sales	Sell products X, Y, Z	Sell 25% more X, Y, Z in first quarter of year	Sales of X, Y, Z by week
Engineering	Make engineering changes to customer orders	Make change and send to production planning 5 days after receiving change request	Engineering changes received by change number and date versus sent to production planning by date
Customer Support	Resolve customer complaint calls	Satisfy immediate call in 15 minutes and have no more than 5% repeat calls	Calls made by day by time to satisfy caller versus return calls
Purchasing	Buy sheet metal raw materials	Buying criteria met by: (a) quantity, (b) delivery date, (c) terms, (d) quality	Sheet metal bought by date by degree of criteria met
Manufacturing	Produce product ABC in cell 5	Make 150 ABCs per takt time and meet quality specs	Hour-by-hour production of ABC and number of defects per part
Inspection	Conduct final inspection on product ABC from cell 5	Inspect every 10th part and provide feedback to cell operators	Hour-by-hour chart inspection of every 10th part and number of defects
Billing	Send invoices and receive cash	Receive cash 30 days after sending invoice	Invoice sent by invoice number versus cash received

FIGURE 10.10
Metrics by department.

3. Testing the hypothesis by implementing the changes
4. Studying the results of the changes and repeating step 2

The kaizen method was taught to the Japanese in post-World War II reconstruction by W. Edwards Deming, under the direction of General Douglas McArthur. The Japanese added their fanaticism for removing waste to the scientific method and Deming contributed the "plan–do–check–act" model.

The resulting kaizen has proven to be a very effective process improvement tool when it is in the hands of:

1. The processes owner directing the kaizen event
2. The process doers conducting the process
3. The process customers and other interested parties observing the process
4. All members in the kaizen studying the process and identifying improvement changes

They make the changes in real time and repeat the process to see how the changes shorten the lead time, reduce errors, and improve first-time quality.

Determining the frequency of kaizens per department will get you started, but the metrics will indicate the processes in the office or shop department that will require improvement using kaizen. But, getting back to the purpose of developing the "Lean management system—departmental governance," it is intended to get you started to determine the breadth and depth of your Lean management system. It is simply a place to start. The next step is to determine how you will go about implementing the system. We have many successes built on many failures that lead us to recommend the hoshin planning and deployment model described previously. As a reminder, hoshin planning is shown again in Figure 10.11.

We will give you some ideas of what your break-through objectives (BTOs), annual tactical actions (ATAs), Gantt chart, and metrics might look like, to get you going on the road to creating your own Lean management system (Figure 10.12). Let us use the name *Made in USA Co.* as the name of your company and assume it will take 3 years to implement your Lean management system fully.

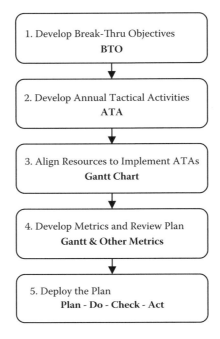

FIGURE 10.11
Hoshin planning model.

The deployed project chart might look like the one in Figure 10.13.

An example of metrics for ATA 1, "educate all employees in Lean," is shown in Figures 10.14 and 10.15.

As you create your Lean management system, Lean principles will guide the behaviors of everyone, starting with the board of directors and on down the line. This will be a significant learning experience for everyone. Of course, the degree of learning will depend upon how closely you currently operate a Lean system. Here are some examples of working in a Lean management system:

- All employees, shop and office, perform their jobs according to standard work.
  - Standard work:
    - Defines how to do the task and the time allowances for the task
      - Will vary depending the repeatability of the task
    - Measurable outcomes of the task
      - Will vary depending on the variability of the task
      - Employees keeping their own measurement boards to track the outcomes
      - Variances noted
- When variances occur that the employee cannot correct, the employee notifies his manager or supervisor.

Break-Through Objective

We Will Create & Implement The

Made In USA Co. Lean Management System in 3 Years

Annual Tactical Activities (ATAs)—Year 1

ATA 1 education		**ATA leader: Adam Caldwell, HR mgr.**
	ATA 1.1	Identify Lean trainer
	ATA 1.2	Develop Lean training program
	ATA 1.3	Train all department managers
	ATA 1.4	Train all employees
ATA 2 standard work		**ATA leader: Ken Franklin, Lean mgr.**
	ATA 2.1	Create standard work teams for each department
	ATA 2.2	Determine standard work for each department
	ATA 2.3	Write standard work for each department
	ATA 2.4	Train employees in using standard work
ATA 3 metrics		**ATA leader: Betty Montgomery, quality mgr.**
	ATA 3.1	Create metrics teams for each department
	ATA 3.2	Determine metrics for each department
	ATA 3.3	Write metrics for each department
	ATA 3.4	Train employees in using metrics

FIGURE 10.12

Break-through objective and annual tactical activities.

- – Together they determine the cause and solve the problem or make a temporary fix until a permanent solution can be made.
- Supervisors, managers, officers of the company, and persons who have a vested interest in the job site make periodic visits to the employees performing the jobs to:
  - Check their job charts
  - Engage in a dialogue with the employee to collect information regarding the job, its standard work, and the outcomes
  - Ask for suggestions the employee has for improvements

This is a very limited example of what it is like to work in a Lean management system, but adjusting to the rigor will be difficult for some personnel, especially the president. It is therefore wise to plan for dealing with these issues, which will certainly occur. Some companies have devised discussion groups of teams, led by a manager or officer of the company, to listen to the concerns employees are having with the change, and to develop

ATA	Action		Person	Est Time	Completion Date				
					Jan	Feb	Mar	Apr	May
ATA 1	**Educate All Employees in Lean**		**Adam**	**440 hr**					
ATA 1.1	Identify Lean trainer	☺	Jack	40 hr	20-Jan				
ATA 1.2	Develop Lean training program	☺	Byron	160 hr			1-Mar		
ATA 1.3	Train all department managers	☹	Harry	40 hr				1-Apr	
ATA 1.4	Train all employees		Bill	200 hr					
ATA 2	**Develop Standard Work for All Departments**		**Ken**	**982 hr**					
ATA 2.1	Create standard work teams for each department		Max	32 hr					
ATA 2.2	Determine standard work for each department		Dave	50 hr					
ATA 2.3	Write standard work for each department		Jenny	800 hr					
ATA 2.4	Train employees in using standard work		Gilda	100 hr					
ATA 3	**Develop Metrics for All Departments**		**Betty**	**332 hr**					
ATA 3.1	Create metrics teams for each department		Mark	32 hr					
ATA 3.2	Determine metrics for each department		Will	50 hr					
ATA 3.3	Write metrics for each department		Sally	200 hr					
ATA 3.4	Train employees in using metrics		Jim	50 hr					

FIGURE 10.13
Project chart.

LEAN TRAINING METRIC								
	Total	Total Trained	Number Trained on Month:					
Department	Personnel	to Date	Jan	Feb	Mar	Apr	May	Jun
Board of Directors	5	4			1	2	1	
President	1	1			1			
VPs	4	2			2			
Managers	5	5			5			
Supervisors	8	8			8			
HR	3	3			3			
Mkt'ing-Dev'l	5	5			3	2		
Mkt'ing-Advs'ing	3	3			2	1		
Sales-Inside	6	6			3	3		
Sales-Outside	12	3			0	1	2	
Eng'ing-Design	5	5			3	2		
Eng'ing-Mfg'ing	6	6			2	3	1	
Warranty	2	2			1	1		
Customer Serv	3	3			1	2		
Purchasing	3	3					1	2
Prod Cnt'l	3	3					0	3
Manufacturing	40	40					20	20
Ship & Rcv'ing	8	8					4	4
Qual Planning	2	2			1	1		
Process Cnt'l	2	2			2			
Inspection	5	5			2	3		
Cost Acct'ing	4	4			4			
Billing	2	2			2			

FIGURE 10.14

Lean training metric for ATA 1.

ways to gain acceptance while continuing to move on with creating the Lean management system.

A principle that has worked for us to gain employee acceptance is to err on the side of more employee involvement than less in designing the system, especially when the design will result in a change that is close to home for the employee. The principle is to involve the employees in the design—for example, the standard work for the job they will be doing, including how the metrics will be designed, even if it is different from what

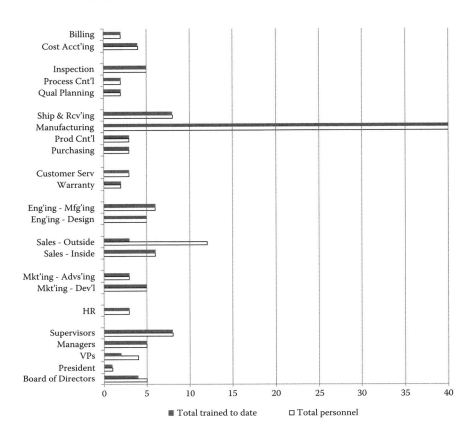

FIGURE 10.15
Lean training chart for ATA 1.

an expert might suggest. There is an old saying that "people hate change, except when it is *their* change." The goal is to achieve the end result, not necessarily how to achieve it. When the employees are engaged, the acceptance of the design will be greater and longer lasting than if an expert said, "Do it this way." Saying that is a sure way to meet with resistance.

Our advice in implementing your Lean management system is to be

- Constantly engaged with your people
- Flexible in its design
- Persistent in moving forward
- Meticulous in its daily implementation
- Continuously making improvements

In summary, we have discussed some of the larger problems and issues you might encounter as you bring your USA 41 back to America.

To ensure you are aware of all the reshoring barriers and roadblocks, we encourage you to continue to engage your people and outside experts. Opening your company's blind spots is best done when everyone is looking outward and feeding information back to the center. It is like in the old western movies: Circling the wagons was the best way to see where the attack might be coming from and then take appropriate action.

We hope the few suggestions, charts, and models will help you to reshore your USA 41 or improve the effectiveness of manufacturing the products you currently are making in America.

REFERENCES

1. Facts about manufacturing in the United States. 2013. National Association of Manufacturers website. http://www.nam.org/Statistics-And-Data/Facts-About-Manufacturing/Landing.aspx
2. Gerry Dick. Differences between right to work states and non-right to work states. Inside Indiana Business with Gerry Dick. http://www.insideindianabusiness.com/contributors.asp?id=1189 (November 2013).
3. Minnesota AFL-CIO. "Right to work" laws: Get the facts. http://www.mnaflcio.org/news/right-work-laws-get-facts (November 2013).

Section VII

Looking into the Future

11

Why It Is Important to Bring American Jobs Back to the United States

MICRO- AND MACROECONOMIC ISSUES

We have talked with many people during the research and writing of this book. They come from all stages of work experience, professional and personal positions, education, age, economic condition, political party, and spiritual belief. There is a common belief among them, regardless of the obvious differences, that we should have more good jobs in America—jobs that pay well, are meaningful, and fulfilling. They also believe that reshoring manufacturing jobs will support the development of good jobs. We could discuss what will happen if we do not bring these good jobs back, but let us take a different approach and talk about will happen when we do—**and we will**—reshore many of our manufacturing jobs back to the United States.

- Manufacturers will hire employees to carry out reshoring their products: engineers, CAD/CAM operators, buyers, clerks, supervisors, machinists, machine operators, equipment repair persons, and general laborers.
- Supply chains will have an increased demand to support manufacturers with materials and services and will hire people to satisfy the demand.
- Small businesses will set up shops to provide personal services to the people working in the factories and offices: restaurants, barber shops, car repair shops, etc.
- Empty buildings will become occupied by the new businesses. They will be improved and provide a pleasant appearance to their streets and blocks.

- Colleges will have greater demand in business management, accounting, and engineering classes. Trade schools will have greater demand in welding, machining, inspection, machine operation, beautician, cooking, and automotive mechanics classes.
- City and state taxes will increase revenue from sales taxes, property taxes, and income taxes. Communities and states will make improvements in their infrastructure. They will attract more businesses with incentives to continue the trend in building tax revenue.
- Communities will prosper.
- Our nation will become stronger and become the economic power that it once was.

Sounds almost too good to be true, does it not? But rebuilding America is what reshoring is all about.

This book's intent is to be a cog in the wheel of the reshoring effort. It is a very brief history of why the offshoring craze began and the changes in global economics that are fostering the reshoring effort. It is also a self-help guide to provide your business leaders with a way to make visible what they otherwise would not see, opening up their blind spots. Additionally, you now have new or, maybe not so new, language to use in your company:

- True unit cost
- Velocity of cash©
- Cash conversion cycle
- Intangible and hidden issues
- SWOT analysis

You have also learned terms, techniques, and models for you to use in making the reshoring a reality:

- Hoshin planning
- Break-through objective
- Annual tactical activity
- Gantt chart
- Project chart
- Plan–do–check–act
- Apprenticeship program
- Basic job skills
- Job diary

- Employee expectations
- Product redesign comparison
- Labor Management Relations Act
- Taft–Hartley Act
- Right-to-work states
- Incentives
- Future and uncertain consequences
- Immediate and certain consequences
- The value stream
- The evil-ings
- Lean tools
- Lean leadership model
- Lean management system
- Standard work—metrics—kaizen
- Circling the wagons

Applying the techniques you are learning will lead your company toward a successful reshoring effort. The techniques will also help you make informed decisions regarding:

- Whether or not to reshore
- Redesigning products for the benefit of all interested departments and customers
- Improving your operational effectiveness by adopting Lean tools
- Improving your total organizational effectiveness by implementing a Lean management system

If you are still uncertain about making the reshoring decision, why not do what the TV commercials suggest, "Ask your doctor [substitute board of directors or advisory board] if reshoring is right for you"? Your board might ask you a few questions, such as "If you reshore:"

- Will you have more control over your manufacturing?
- Will your products be built better?
- Will you have more control over your intellectual property?
- Will you be able to make changes faster?
- Will you get your products faster to market?
- Will you have a "made in America" label on your products?

- Will your customers feel better about your products if they are "made in America"?
- Will your customers buy more of your products?
- Will your employees feel better about your company?
- Will productivity increase?
- Will your sales increase?
- Will your margins increase?
- Will your cash flow be faster?
- Will your company be more profitable?
- What will your reshoring investment be? $ ____
- What will your ROI be? $ ____

These are the microeconomic questions you must deal with to ensure your company is profitable and remains profitable. At the end of the day, you must have more revenue than expenses, more in the *black* than in the *red*. How much more *black* than *red* is a decision you must make, another question you must answer. It reminds one of the story of the goose that laid the golden eggs. A poor farmer and his wife were blessed one day with a goose that laid golden eggs, but it laid only one golden egg each day. The farmer and his wife were lifted out of poverty and lived a very comfortable life. They were now out of the *red* and in the *black*. Then the farmer and his wife asked the question, "How much more *black* do we want to have?" and the answer came back, "Even more!" So the farmer and his wife decided to get all the eggs from the goose at one time. Taking a knife, they cut open the goose to retrieve the eggs, only to discover that on the inside, the goose was as normal as any other. They killed the goose, and it laid no more golden eggs. The farmer and his wife were soon in the *red* again.

The story is as old as Aesop, and it reminds us about temperance and what consequences its absence might reap. The goose in this context is a metaphor for those things that support your business's very existence. The goose represents your employees, your customers and their ability to pay, your supply chain, your community, and your country.

These are the macroeconomic issues that you impact, either directly or indirectly, and they, in turn, impact you and your business. The offshoring movement was intended to improve companies' microeconomic positions, and in some cases it did, at first. However, as time went by businesses became savvier about the downside of offshoring and the "goose" became anemic, which brought us to our current state of affairs. It is obvious that all business leaders have a responsibility to maximize their companies' microeconomic position. But, they also must have a responsibility to maximize our collective macroeconomic condition. It is the only way to keep the goose healthy for all of us to reap its fruits.

To move further toward the decision whether to reshore or not, ask these questions:

"If we reshore, will we be *contributing* to:"

- Creating more jobs in America?
- Rebuilding the supply chain in America?
- Encouraging young people to be interested in tinkering with how things are made?
- Rejuvenating lost skills in America?
- Encouraging young people to find summer and part-time jobs?
- Providing our young people with more job opportunities?
- Putting fewer Americans on welfare?
- Increasing the number of Americans paying taxes?
- Reducing our national debt?
- Making our communities better places to live, work, and raise a family?
- Adding to products with the "made in America" label?
- Returning the work ethic to America?
- Making America a better country?
- Making America a stronger country?
- Making you even more proud to say, "I am an American"?

If you answered these macroeconomic questions in the affirmative and if the answers to microeconomic questions say you are in a favorable business condition, you are probably on your way to making the decision to reshore. Regardless of how large or small your reshoring will be, there is always comfort in knowing that others, the pioneers, have gone before you. Their stories and experiences might make the final decision easier for you.

RESHORING PIONEERS

Many business leaders are in the process of making the reshoring decision or already have made it. Those who have made the decision are certainly reshoring pioneers. These pioneers blazed the trail and paved the way for others to see their trials and errors in reaching their goals, to make their companies more profitable and effective, and to make America the economic power it once was. They most likely went through the same ordeals you are experiencing or will experience as you make your reshoring decision by:

- Asking many questions
- Receiving many different answers
- Sorting out the right answers from the wrong
- Dealing with conflicting priorities
- Searching for resources
- Questioning your own decisions
- Having others question your decisions
- Losing lots of sleep

Although the road to reshoring was not an easy one for them, just like our forefathers and foremothers as they moved from the east coast of America to the west, the fruits of success were ultimately worth the effort…for those who made it! This book was written to be your guide as you make the journey so that you *will* make it, and to give you encouragement and to show you that others have made it. Here are a few of their reshoring pioneer stories.

Element Electronics

A manufacturer of large flat-screen TVs in Detroit, Michigan, Element Electronics[1] made the decision to reshore what they could of TV production. Even though television components have not been made in the United States for years, their president, Mike O'Shaughnessy, made the decision to assemble their new, larger size televisions in America to, as he said, "Give… customers a great out-of-the-box experience with the TVs having the label *assembled in America*."

His decision was based on the costs being essentially the same for assembling their TVs in the United States as in China because of:

- Shortened supply chains
- Reduced lead time
- Ability to control waste
- Improved quality
- Eliminated import duty
- Avoidance of transcontinental shipping costs

He also felt that, by assembling the TVs in the United States, he could:

- Apply what he calls "global localization"—assembling TVs closer to where they will be sold
- Take advantage of a local qualified labor pool
- Be more responsive to changes in demand and the desire for new features

President O'Shaughnessy also wanted to do his part in returning manufacturing to America. In the 1950s there were 150 companies making televisions in America; today there are virtually none. Mike put it very well when he said: "We have watched for years as jobs have left America for other countries. We have wanted to and planned for producing TVs here, at home. Element Electronics wants to pioneer a resurgence of creating quality manufacturing jobs in the USA."

The Outdoor GreatRoom Company

Founded by brothers Dan and Ron Shimek, The Outdoor GreatRoom Company[2] is a dream come true. Their vision has been to give homeowners two living rooms, one indoors and one outdoors, where they and their guests can experience a relaxing environment of both worlds. Their company, in Minnesota, builds fire pits, fire places, pergolas, outdoor kitchens, and lighting. Most of the Outdoor GreatRoom Company's products were made in China. In 2010, Dan and Ron made the decision to begin bringing their products back from China.

As Dan, CEO of the company, said about bringing their products back to America:

> First and foremost, it gives us the opportunity to have a majority of our products be American made. Not only does this improve the speed in which we can get our products to our customers, it consolidates all of our operations under one location. We now don't have to account for shipping lags or quality control which has started to become a growing concern in the China manufacturing arena.

Dan and Ron also are proud about contributing to the US economy by bringing their jobs back. Dan said:

> There is a pride aspect of being a US company and being able to say that you are employing Americans to produce your products especially at a time where job growth has been nonexistent. It feels so much better, to be able to accomplish the same manufacturing goals, with Americans producing our products.

Simplicity

A division of Tacony Manufacturing, Simplicity[3] makes vacuum cleaners in St. James, Missouri. Simplicity is one of hundreds of vacuum cleaner brands. It must compete every day on price, quality, and meeting customer expectations. A few years ago Bill Hinderer, president of Simplicity, thought he could compete better if he brought his vacuum cleaners back from Korea and China to his plant in Missouri. Since he made the decision to reshore,

Simplicity's employment at the St. James plant has grown from 45 to 120 employees—a 167% increase!

In a TV feature, produced by CBS's Channel 4 KMOV in St. Louis, commentator Larry Conners interviewed president Bill Hinderer on the Simplicity manufacturing floor. The segment is called "Simplicity Vacuum—Made in the USA." Here is some dialogue from the show:

- "We're working in the heartland to build world class vacuums."
- "Simplicity is making their vacuums in America when others are saying they can't."
- "Made in America is a strong selling point; the company promotes it with labels and packaging."
- "Simplicity has proved that goods can be made in America and at competitive prices."
- "We would like to see more businesses do the same."
- "I think as we can show success and [if] Channel 4 publishes that, then I think other people will certainly think of it."

Suarez Industries

Suarez Industries[4,5] is a direct marketing company based in Canton, Ohio. It makes a wide variety of products like jewelry, collectable coins, household products, and health supplements. Suarez Industries was founded by Ben Suarez, an entrepreneur and savvy businessman who cares about growing his company and his community. He has developed business learning centers at the University of Akron and works closely with his community in Canton. Ben decided it was time to move production of his high-performance EdenLine space heater from China to Canton. Hope Paolini, the operations manager at the EdenLine manufacturing plant, was given the task of finding ways to manufacture the space heaters in Canton more cost effectively so that they could be reshored from China. Hope applied low-tech methods to reduce the labor cost of the heaters. She and her staff redesigned the heater so that it required fewer screws and almost no rivets, so fewer workers were needed to assemble the product. The results of her efforts are inspiring to all reshoring advocates:

- 450 new jobs at the Canton factory
- 13 new jobs for suppliers of power cords
- 20 new jobs for sheet metal stampers
- 18 new jobs for plastic molding suppliers

When asked why everybody is not reshoring, Hope Paolini had this answer: "It's easier to say, 'It can't be done' than to get up early and to work hard and to make it happen."

Ben Suarez is now considering reintroducing vacuum cleaner production at his Canton facility.

WHAM-O*

WHAM-O[6] has been making fun products the whole world has known and played with for over 65 years: Hula Hoop, Slip'N-Slide, Super Ball, Hacky Sack, Boogie Board, but most of all (...drum roll, please...) Frisbee! Who has not spun a Frisbee™ when a kid, or kid at heart? It is sad to know that most of WHAM-O's products are made offshore, but recently, at least two of their products are being reshored to America: PoolZone and Frisbees. WHAM-O has teamed up with Manufacturing Marvel America, a division of the international Manufacturing Marvel Group that specializes in plastic injection molding, to produce its Frisbees.

When asked about Frisbees being reshored back to America, WHAM-O CEO Kyle Aguilar says:

- "The main reason is cost of production."
- "We are making progress toward our goal of producing half of all Frisbee discs in the United States."

There is also talk of reshoring Hula Hoop production back to the United States. WHAM-O has a formally stated "corporate social responsibility" with a mission to "help kids and families from all around the world to enjoy life." Their social responsibility extends to helping America become economically strong again. As CEO Aguilar said about reshoring Frisbees: "We're proud to help stimulate the local job market by bringing more manufacturing jobs back to the US."

Michigan Ladder Company

Michigan Ladder Company[7] has been making wooden ladders in Ypsilanti, Michigan, since 1901. Over the decades, the company produced other products such as ironing boards, boats, and its famous ping pong table named *The Detroiter*. It was used by the Harlem Globetrotters during halftimes for entertainment and by Tom Hanks in the movie *Forrest Gump*. Michigan Ladder returned to its core competency, making wooden ladders, and added aluminum and fiberglass ladders to its line. Wooden ladders had always been fully made at the Ypsilanti plant, but fiberglass ladders were imported from China and resold to customers and industrial clients. Since fiberglass ladders account for half of the company's sales, Tom Harrison, the president of Michigan Ladder, made the decision to see if they could be made better and more economically in house.

Tom says the following about making the reshoring decision:

> With advances in technology and high freight costs, it's the perfect time to begin marketing an American-made product. China's wages are going up, diesel fuel for shipping costs is getting more expensive, and government support for industries in China will go away over time. You'll see more manufacturing coming back here over time, but we just decided we're not going to wait.

The company is sourcing fiberglass from its supply chain and assembling the ladders in house. Several new jobs have been created. Tom said he could add even more jobs when his supply chain keeps up with his production.

Tom has high hopes for Michigan Ladder: "For the foreseeable future, I think it's a safe bet that we would stay here and continue to expand here in Ypsilanti as much as we can."

Hopefully these pioneers have given you the encouragement and confidence that reshoring *can* be done. Please note the duality of the comments each business leader made of the economic value reshoring brings to his company and his concern for our country. Their words should be a reminder to consider both the micro- and macroeconomic issues when making the reshoring decision. The relationship between business and country is an interlocking symbiotic relationship; our businesses and our country are dependent upon each other. One without the other makes it difficult for either to survive.

The question is, "What do you do now?"

NEXT STEPS FOR YOU

Giving advice is always a thorny proposition. Advice is usually steeped in beliefs, motivation, and experiences. The best way for you to decide if you want to listen to our advice is for us to be up front with our beliefs, motivations, and experiences. Then you can make the decision if you want to take our advice. Here, now, are the beliefs, motivations, and expertise of your authors, Tim Hutzel and Dave Lippert.

Our Beliefs

- We believe that work is fundamentally good and should be sought after by us, God's children. Work is blessed by God in numerous scripture verses:
  - Psalm 90:17 "May the favor of the Lord our God rest on us; establish the work of our hands for us—yes, establish the work of our hands."
  - Deuteronomy 15:10 "Give generously to them and do so without a grudging heart; then because of this the Lord your God will

bless you in all your work and in everything you put your hand to."

- We believe the responsibility of business leaders is to maximize the effectiveness of their businesses while at the same time being socially responsible to their communities and America.
- We believe the offshoring of American manufacturing jobs was well intended by business leaders and driven more by the desire to survive or increase their financial profitability but at the expense of their communities and America.
- We believe America has been weakened economically, as demonstrated by our excessive national debt and lack of tax base to cover it.
- We believe America has the ability to recover from offshoring if its leaders have the will, information, resources, and stamina that it will require.

Our Motivation

- We are motivated to make America the economic power it once was by presenting methodologies that will assist business leaders to make the reshoring decision and improve the effectiveness of their businesses.
- We are motivated to work one on one with business leaders and their employees to make their reshoring a reality.
- We are motivated to cooperate with state and community officials to spread the word of reshoring to their constituents and how to accomplish a reshoring effort. Officials could be: governors, mayors, council persons, economic development directors, chamber of commerce leaders, professional societies, etc.

Our Experience

- We have worked in all phases of manufacturing for a combined total of 75 years. We have:
  - Worked in factories alongside machinists, welders, laborers, painters, metal pourers, mold makers, inspectors, and many others
  - Supported manufacturing by working in these roles: design engineer, manufacturing engineer, process control engineer, quality control engineer, production control engineer
  - Managed manufacturing operations in these management roles: quality manager, manufacturing manager, tool room supervisor,

shop supervisor, inventory supervisor, inspection supervisor, vice president of organizational effectiveness, president of the company
- Taught and coached manufacturing companies to improve their total operational effectiveness in these product families: industrial casters, travel trailers, power transmissions, transformers and motors, fluid valves, armored trucks, heavy-duty trucks, aircraft engines, home-building products, food products, medical devices, and jet aircraft and components
- Promoted and written about bringing manufacturing jobs back to America

Now that you know our beliefs, motivation, and experience, you have probably decided whether or not to keep reading and let us advise you on next steps. So here goes, categorized by who you might be:

To Community Leaders

Talk with your constituents about reshoring, perhaps at one of your regular functions. Share with them what you have learned when manufacturing jobs are offshored and the effects it has had on the community and local businesses—for example:

- For every $1.00 lost in local manufacturing, another $1.48 lost to the community
- Lost manufacturing jobs—unemployment—people leaving town to find work
- Lost opportunities for young people—not getting part-time jobs—hanging out
- Reduced tax base—city services being neglected
- Reduced retail income—storefronts closing
- Tax levies for schools, fire departments, police forces voted "NO!"—community services decline
- Difficult to persuade new families to settle in the community

Encourage your manufacturing constituents to understand the pitfalls of offshoring their manufacturing:

- Differences of cultures and language
- Wages rising in China

- Shipping costs escalating
- Long lead times
- High order quantity
- Risk of spoilage and obsolescence
- Inability to control production and quality
- True unit cost higher than initially thought
- Velocity of Cash—slow
- Cash conversion cycle—long
- Customers desiring "made in America" label

Encourage them to seek professional assistance to see if reshoring is for them and, if so, to reshore their manufacturing back to the United States.

To Economic Development Directors

Do much of the same as the community leaders, but take the conversation with your manufacturing constituents to a deeper level, such as:

- Show them the Reshoring Decision-Making Model© as shown again in Figure 11.1.
- Help them to follow the steps in phases I and II or have them call for professional assistance with the task.

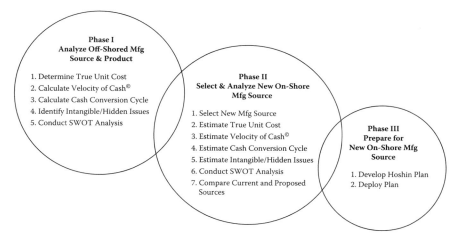

FIGURE 11.1
Reshoring Decision-Making Model.©

- Encourage them to continue with phase III if the results from phases I and II show it will be favorable to reshore.

To Religious Leaders

As a topic of a Saturday or Sunday sermon, do much of the same as we suggest to the community leaders, but take a religious slant to the topic. Remind your congregation about the Godliness and goodness of work and how the offshoring of American manufacturing jobs, to far away countries, has reduced opportunities for American men and women to find meaningful work. Perhaps cite scripture verses and weave them into daily lives—for example:

- Proverbs 16:3 "Commit your work to the Lord, and your plans will be established."
- Proverbs 10:4 "A slack hand causes poverty, but the hand of the diligent makes rich."
- Proverbs 12:11 "Whoever works his land will have plenty of bread, but he who follows worthless pursuits lacks sense."
- Leviticus 23:22 "When you reap the harvest of your land, do not reap to the very edges of your field or gather the gleanings of your harvest. Leave them for the poor and the alien. I am the Lord your God."

Discover those in your congregation who have been affected by offshoring and learn the stories they might have about the topic of offshoring and how it relates to their personal lives.

Inform your congregation about the reshoring movement and the good news that reshoring is becoming the trend, albeit slowly, and to pray for those involved in reshoring.

To Manufacturing Leaders

We hope that by the time we arrive at this place in our book, our advice is obvious. As they say, *as plain as the nose on your face* and *as subtle as a brick wall*. Of course we want you to reshore, but only if it makes sense to you. That is the theme of this book: to help you make an informed decision, to see if reshoring makes sense to you. We designed our models to be inclusive, so that you have the advantage of hearing everyone's input on what offshoring has done to your company and what reshoring might look like. We then went outside the boundaries of your company asking you to consider the impact a reshoring decision could have on your community and America. We understand your obligation to maximize your economic resources to make your company profitable because we have both been, and still are, business owners. God only knows how we understand! But the fact remains that we believe we need to turn the negative societal and macroeconomic effects of offshoring around. So here is our advice:

- Read the book again. Make notes in the margins, turn the corners over on the pages you feel are important, highlight important passages, make notes on a separate tablet, etc.
- Share the book and your thoughts with your *community leaders*. Get their opinions.
- Share the book and your thoughts with your *economic development leaders*. Get their opinions.
- Share the book and your thoughts with your *religious leaders*. Get their opinions.
- Share the book and your thoughts with your *staff*. Get their opinions.
- If there is a "go" decision to explore reshoring or to explore keeping your manufacturing in America, find an expert in reshoring and facilitation who can lead you through the Reshoring Decision-Making Model.

Go with your eyes wide open and make the best decision for:
  - Your company
  - Your employees
  - Your customers
  - Your community
  - America

FINAL COMMENTS

If we seem to you like reshoring fanatics, we apologize. On the other hand, if you believe we are enthusiastic about bringing jobs back to America, then we are flattered. We hope that we have given you, whether you are a young person, manufacturing leader, parent, chamber of commerce president, economic development director, pastor, rabbi, or just an interested person, a new look at what has been happening in American manufacturing since the offshoring surge. We also hope that we have struck a chord with you for the need to reshore manufacturing and reverse the domino effects of offshoring and what it has done to our country and society.

We want to apologize for any toes that we may have stepped on, especially those who persuaded their companies to offshore, the accountants and financial gurus. Pursuit of financial gain was their duty, but the totality of offshoring consequences was unknown to them. We hold them responsible but ignorant; they should have had more complete data. We also apologize to companies that had no choice in offshoring, like Huffy Bicycles, which was helpless when China dumped bicycles on the American market at prices that were lower than even the cost of making them in China!

We are less apologetic, however, to our nation's lawmakers, who seem more interested in their personal agendas than the greater good of America and its citizens. It is unbelievable that collective Washington has not done its share to make "made in America" easier. American manufacturers must put up with the highest tax structure in the world and deal with the renegade shenanigans of federal regulatory agencies. For example, in 2013 the head of the EPA said that he would "crucify" oil and gas companies to make examples of them. Makes you proud to be an American, does it not?

In parting, we hope that you are more informed about reshoring and want to do your share in creating more products that have the label that we all want to see: "made in America."

Good luck and God bless,

Tim Hutzel and Dave Lippert

REFERENCES

1. Melissa Kubrin and Shara Koplowitz. Element Electronics brings back TV manufacturing to the United States with the opening of their factory in Detroit, Michigan. PRNewswire. http://m.prnewswire.com/news-releases/element-electronics-america-matters-137021908.html (January 10, 2012).
2. Outdoor GreatRoom Company creates jobs and increases quality by bringing manufacturing back to Minnesota. PRWEB. khttp://www.prweb.com/releases/prweb2011/10/prweb8879612.htm (October 17, 2011).
3. Larry Conners. *Good news 4 a Change.* Segment: Simplicity vacuum—Made in the USA. CBS TV Station KMOV, St. Louis, April 3, 2009.
4. Jim Axelrod. Applying Yankee ingenuity to bring home US jobs. *CBS Evening News.* http://www.cbsnews.com/news/applying-yankee-ingenuity-to-bring-home-us-jobs/ (March 1, 2012).

5. Robert Schoenberger. Are manufacturing jobs coming back to United States? *The Plain Dealer.* http://www.cleveland.com/business/index.ssf/2013/03/reshoring_conference_to_study.html (March 9, 2013).
6. WHAM-O brings Frisbee production to the US. Emeryville, CA (PRWEB). http://www.prweb.com/releases/WHAMO/frisbeeproduction/prweb3412684.htm (January 6, 2010).
7. Lizzy Alfs. Michigan Ladder Co. expanding Ypsilanti manufacturing operation in shift away from foreign suppliers. *The Ann Arbor News.* http://annarbor.com/business-review/michigan-ladder-co-expanding-ypsilanti-manufacturing-operation-in-shift-away-from-foreign-suppliers/ (September 11, 2011).

Index

About the Authors

Tim Hutzel was born into a blue-collar family in a very small town in southwestern Ohio in 1945. His parents were Depression-era folk who survived by watching their pennies and working hard. Tim entered the workforce at age 14 doing odd jobs such as washing pots and pans at a neighborhood restaurant, operating kiddy rides at a small amusement park, delivering papers, and performing light factory work. Three years later, Tim joined the US Army at age 17 as a volunteer and learned the fine art of field artillery; he spent three years in West Germany helping keep the Russians on the east side of the Berlin Wall. Fifty plus years later Tim has accrued experiences that include three university degrees, 21 years employment at GE Aviation, 20 years self-employment helping businesses improve themselves, writing a book on how American companies can survive in the United States, serving as adjunct professor to Miami University's College of Engineering and Computing and the Farmer School of Business. And now, Tim has written this book with his good friend, Dave Lippert. Tim's age says retirement, but his actions prove differently; he continues to be involved with American businesses, helping them improve their operations and profitability.

Dave Lippert grew up in southwestern Ohio in an industrious family that founded a manufacturing business in 1907, making and selling industrial casters, wheels, and carts. Currently, Hamilton Caster is in its fourth generation of family management. Dave spent his summers working in the family business and experiencing the sights, sounds, and smells of the manufacturing floor. He earned his engineering degree at the US Air Force Academy and after serving 6 years in the Air Force, returned to Hamilton Caster to work under his dad, then the president. In 1995 Dave succeeded his father to become the company's fifth president, the position he now holds. Dave led his company to adopt the Toyota production system philosophy by creating the Hamilton Caster management system, a spin-off of what is commonly known as a Lean management system. In 1996, Hamilton Caster was awarded first place among Ohio small businesses for team excellence based on early experiences with Lean. Dave is unwaveringly dedicated to his family, church, company, community, and helping American businesses reach their full potential.